Space for God

Study and Practice of Spirituality and Prayer

DON POSTEMA

FAITH
ALIVE®
Christian Resources

Grand Rapids, Michigan

Cover art: Three Willows at Sunset, Vincent Van Gogh
Rijksmuseum Kröller-Müller, Otterlo, Netherlands/
Bridgeman Art Library, London/Superstock

Back cover photo: © Paula Christensen, Ann Arbor, Michigan

Library of Congress Cataloging-in-Publication Data

Postema, Donald H., 1934-
    Space for God.

    Bibliography: p.
    1. Spiritual life. 2. Prayer. 3. Devotional literature.
4. Postema, Donald H., 1934-   I. Title. II. Series.
BV4501.2.P5565   1983   248.3   83-15504
ISBN 978-0-933140-46-2

A Leader's Guide for this book is also available.

12 11 10 9 8 7 6 5

CONTENTS

PREFACE

In this book Don Postema offers us a space to live gratefully in the presence of God. He gives us his personal spiritual journey, his experience in the Christian ministry, his wide interest in art and literature, and most of all his own hospitable personality as the space in which we, who read this book, can listen fearlessly to God's voice. The way Don has organized this book shows its hospitality: each chapter contains his own reflections, a wide variety of quotations that function as windows to insight, exercises to help us practice what we have learned, and encouragement to fill the empty pages of a personal journal with notes on our own journey. Thus the book does what it describes: it creates space for God.

I cannot think of a better way to introduce this book than to follow Don's own method. First I want to offer a few reflections on the unique quality of this book, then I plan to take a look through the windows to insight, and finally I would like to write some notes on the empty pages. I won't offer any exercises!

I. This book is inviting because it is personal. Don has not hesitated to offer his own exuberant personality as a guide into the territory of the spiritual life. Against the background of his own unique life, he witnesses to the vital presence of God within and among us. The result is a refreshing presentation of a Calvinistic spirituality. During the sabbatical year that Don spent at Yale Divinity School he discovered intimate connections between the writings of his own spiritual father, John Calvin, and the words of many great spiritual fathers of other Christian traditions. This discovery made it possible for Don to develop a spirituality deeply rooted in his own religious heritage while open to many influences that at first seemed foreign. What has emerged from this process of connecting and reconnecting is a spirituality of gratitude.

I find it very striking that this book has become an expression of and a call to gratitude. Don is a profoundly grateful person. Gratitude is one of his most visible characteristics. This not only has made my friendship with him a joyful experience but also has made me come to a deeper appreciation of John Calvin's theology of sanctification, the theology that forms the basis of Don's spirituality.

II. The windows to insight that Don opens for us are as attractive as they are unusual. Drawings by Rembrandt, Vincent Van Gogh, Yushi Nomura; quotations from Scripture, theologians, monks, and poets; and songs from a variety of origins—they all show us new ways of living gratefully in the house of God. Personally I am deeply moved by the evocative way in which Vincent Van Gogh has become present in this book on the spiritual life. Few people would ever think of "the man who cut off his ear" as a guide to God. But those who work with this book will come to know that this Dutch artist not only once was a minister who preached God's Word to the poor but also remained a minister through his letters, drawings, and paintings. I am grateful to Don Postema for placing this controversial Dutchman in the same book with John Calvin.

III. Finally a few notes on the empty pages. God gathers, reconciles, unites. God wants all people who search for him to be one in him through his Son Jesus Christ. Reading Don's book, I came to realize that it is an invitation to unity through prayer, especially through the prayer of gratitude. What else can make us one but prayer? What else can unite us but a common recognition that all that is, is a divine gift calling forth from us words and actions of thanks? What else can gather us but a spirituality of gratitude that sets us free from our many divisions and allows us to celebrate together the presence of the living Christ among us? Don has brought together John Calvin and Thomas Merton; Dutch and Japanese drawings; Protestant, Roman Catholic, and Orthodox reflections. What unites them? Gratitude, the deep awareness of the giftedness of life. The prayer of thanks is indeed the place where we all can meet—not looking at each other and finding fault with each other but looking together at him who forgives us our faults over and again.

When Don came to Yale Divinity School for a year of study, he was searching for an authentic spirituality within his own tradition. Now, a few years later, we have a book that was born there. In this book Don gives more than he received. That is the mystery of gratitude. What is accepted with thanksgiving multiplies in the sharing of it with others. Five loaves and two fishes, received as a gift, were enough to feed a multitude of people. *Space for God* is a hopeful sign of this mystery of gratitude.

—Henri J. M. Nouwen

AN INVITATION

I like this story of St. Sarapion the Sindonite, a Desert Father of fourth-century Egypt. He

> *travelled once on pilgrimage to Rome. Here he was told of a celebrated recluse, a woman who lived always in one small room, never going out. Sceptical about her way of life—for he was himself a great wanderer—Sarapion called on her and asked: "Why are you sitting here?" To this she replied: "I am not sitting. I am on a journey."*
>
> —Told by Fr. Kallistos Ware in *The Orthodox Way,* p. 7

We are all on a journey, a spiritual pilgrimage. Whether we are wanderers or sitters, we are on the Way (Acts 19:23). You are. I am. And now our journeys meet for a short time in this book. I have written it with the hope that it will provide a little guidance and encouragement to explorers of spirituality and prayer—the "heart in pilgrimage" (George Herbert).

I recognize how busy people are. I myself am much more a "wanderer" than a "sitter," more gregarious than introspective, more busy than patient and laid-back, more "extrovert" than "introvert." I wondered whether such a person could be quiet, contemplative, prayerful and could carry that prayerful attitude into the busyness and noisiness of life.

Then I got to know Henri Nouwen.

I was granted a sabbatical by Campus Chapel to pursue study in what I called "Toward a Reformed Understanding of Spirituality." I am very grateful to the church for that year of study and exploration, for it was an experience that deeply affected my life. My sabbatical journey took me to conferences, retreats, monasteries, books, and conversations with wanderers and sitters. More importantly, I was able to study at Yale Divinity School in New Haven, Connecticut. There I renewed my friendship with Father Henri J. M. Nouwen, a fellow Dutchman. Henri was like a hurricane of activity. And it was from him I learned that even hassled and harried people can have a deep spiritual center, a continuing life of prayer and contemplation, and a creative relationship with God. I had read many of his books, but now took courses, listened to lectures, and spent time in stimulating conversation. His inspiration has been invaluable. So many of his words and thoughts have become my own, that I'm sure they have crept into what I have written without proper recognition and will be spotted by those who know him. I can only express my deepest appreciation. His continued interest in this book emphasizes what a generous and lasting friend he is. Before I left New Haven, he and his assistant at Yale, John Mogabgab, inspired me and gave me helpful suggestions as I developed a "spirituality of gratitude."

Colleagues, friends, and members of Campus Chapel also encouraged me to articulate and share what I had learned. How grateful I am to them for urging me to continue exploring a Reformed spirituality in much more depth. Campus Chapel generously gave me the freedom and support to teach and write, to give numerous retreats, seminars, lectures, and sermons. I also deeply appreciate the patient help of the staff, editors, and artist that at last brought *Space for God* to publication.

Finally I thank my family for accompanying me on my journey. How grateful I am that Elaine, my wife, has been willing to share and to risk this pilgrimage—and the writing about it. What a patient fellow traveler in life and in prayer she has been! During the writing of this book, the earthly journey of my father, another Henry, ended. He knows now the joy of perpetually being in the presence of God and is constantly aware of the splendor of our gracious Parent, a splendor we only glimpse. He and my mother, Anna (without whom I never would have begun the journey!), have been a support in my artistic and theological pursuits.

To these last three loving persons—my wife, my father, and my mother—this book is gratefully dedicated.

Donald H. Postema

Pentecost 1983

THE JOURNEY CONTINUES

When *Space for God* was published in 1983, I never dreamed that my journey would intersect with the journeys of so many people who not only bought the book but read it—and even tried to follow some of the suggestions! They've responded with encouraging remarks, personal experiences, and suggestions. This revision takes those suggestions into account. The basic text has not been substantially changed but past mistakes have been corrected, some readings have been added or rearranged, and newer versions of the Bible have been included. I've also added a few spiritual exercises that I've found useful as I continue to give courses and retreats on spirituality and prayer.

It's a mystery to me that something squeezed from my brain, my pain, my joy, and my heart would touch the experience of so many others. How stimulating and enriching to interact with people from various denominations and religious traditions from West Africa to Japan, from Malaysia to Mexico, from Canada to Costa Rica, and from all parts of the United States. Their warm response has been an overwhelming experience for which I am profoundly grateful.

My journey took me to the Vincent Van Gogh Museum in Amsterdam where *Space for God* is on the library shelf. The curator graciously invited me into the vault to view the drawings included in this book. In a visit to the Ecumenical Community of Taizé, France, I found music and a meditative

10

style of worship that deepened my spiritual life, enhanced my teaching of *Space for God,* and has become an integral part of my ministry.

My journey also took me not only to places and persons I never dreamed of but also to deeper places in my own heart. I have found that "belonging to God" *is* a very basic spiritual experience as well as a theological concept, not only for Christians in the Reformed tradition but in other traditions as well. And a "spirituality of gratitude" also connects with people of many traditions in many places.

This journey of befriending many deeply spiritual people has deepened my own friendship with God. In fact, I've come to believe that being a friend of God is a deeper basis for spirituality and prayer than being a servant or even a child of God. I've developed this theme in a new book called *Catch Your Breath* (CRC Publications).

All these experiences have changed my life and given me a new focus for the future. They have influenced my decision to move from a campus ministry to a ministry of giving retreats, conferences, and spiritual direction. Once again, I am grateful to Campus Chapel for the support given to me over thirty-four years to explore and expand my ministry in the direction God seemed to be leading.

A clergy friend once said to me, "I hope you can *do* what you've written about." What a challenge! It made me realize I'm still very much on the journey. I'm honored that you've joined me on this journey as we try to live as friends of God.

I close with a few thoughts about my friend Henri Nouwen, author of the preface to this book. I remember how deeply moved I was when I first received the preface from him. He had caught the essence of my book and expanded gratitude further than I had thought—into a basis of reconciliation and unity. I remember thinking that the preface was the best part of the book! I remember how we shared a passion for Vincent Van Gogh and how Henri had enlarged my understanding of the spirituality of his art so that it found a place in this book. Even the title of this book—*Space for God*—came from Henri. While I was studying with him, he had written a book he called *Space for God,* but his publishers had rejected the title. When I asked him if I could use his title for my book, he said yes!

Little did I realize that on September 21, 1996, the very day I was contemplating his words and putting them into a sermon for the next morning, Henri had died of a massive heart attack. I found out two days later. What a loss! Yet what an inspiration to know this beloved friend of God as our friend. What a gift he was and is to people around the world who are on the journey with the Spirit.

In gratitude, this revision is dedicated to the memory of my friend and mentor, Henri Nouwen.

Donald H. Postema

Epiphany 1997

. . . AND CONTINUES

As I continue on the spiritual journey, I realize more and more that it is not about a destination but about a relationship. It is not about striving to get to God someplace in the future. It is more about being with God, who is persistently present with us. We do not travel alone. The risen Christ is our constant companion on the way, as he was with Cleopas and his wife on the way to Emmaus. His Spirit is always present to comfort, cajole, care, challenge, instruct, encourage, and inspire us on the path of holiness ("sanctification").

Our role is to recognize Jesus, to pay attention to the Divine Presence, to be conscious of God on the way. *Space for God* was written as a guide along the way to cultivating such a God-conscious life. It is an invitation to a spirituality and prayer that "draws down the attention of the mind into the heart . . . [and] with the mind firmly established in the heart, stands before the Lord with awe, reverence, and devotion" (Theophane the Recluse). That perspective influenced my writing. How surprising that something conceived in the heart and mind can travel down the arm and come out of the fingers with words on a page! John Henry Cardinal Newman expressed it for me: "I pray best at the end of my pen." I remember writing the first draft with pencil so it seemed more like drawing: a rough sketch that little by little, by filling in with a thought or experience, pondering and reworking the material, became a portrait of the spiritual life.

However, once the words are written, printed, and published, they become like freeze-dried experience. Until readers immerse them in the warmth of their own experience and they come alive again. Until the Spirit waters them with inspiration, like hot water poured on tea for a refreshing brew.

The book has taken on a life of its own; for almost twenty-five years it has been on a journey around the world . . . even speaking Russian. It seems to have a ministry of its own. Or is it the Divine Companion who has a ministry through it?

It is still a mystery to me that so many people have chosen *Space for God* as one of their guides to accompany them on the spiritual journey. This has confirmed and deepened my conviction that a spirituality of grace, gratitude, and compassion that is at the heart of the Reformed faith can touch the heart of other people of faith. I simply have observed all this with surprise and gratitude. Meister Eckhardt once said that if you come to the end of your life and the only prayer you have uttered is "Thank You," that is enough.

As this new printing goes out on its journey, I continue to say "Thank You"—to you readers who have made that possible, to the publishers who trust the process . . . but especially to God, who is full of surprises and, I imagine, has a few more surprises in store for us on the way.

Donald H. Postema

Easter 2007

12

CHAPTER 1

MAKING SPACE

I must grasp life at its depth.

—Vincent Van Gogh, The Complete Letters, 197, I, 365

*Be still before the L*ORD
and wait patiently for him.

—Psalm 37:7, NRSV

What do you believe when you say:
"I believe in God the Father, Almighty,
Maker of heaven and earth"?

That the eternal Father of our Lord Jesus Christ,
who out of nothing created heaven and earth
and everything in them,
who still upholds and rules them
by his eternal counsel and providence,
is my God and Father
because of Christ his Son.

I trust him so much that I do not doubt
he will provide
whatever I need
for body and soul,
and he will turn to my good
whatever adversity he sends me
in this sad world.

He is able to do this because he is almighty God,
he desires to do it because he is a faithful Father.

—Heidelberg Catechism, Q & A 26

Bent Figure of a Woman

—Vincent Van Gogh

REFLECTION

"Do any human beings ever realize life while they live it—every, every minute?" Emily, a young woman in Thornton Wilder's play *Our Town* asks that question.

In the play Emily dies in childbirth but is granted a unique experience: the Stage Manager allows her to return from death and live one day of her life with her family. Although Emily has high hopes for that one day, she is disappointed. Just before she returns to her place in the cemetery, she reveals her frustration to the Stage Manager:

> Emily: *We don't have time to look at one another.* (She breaks down, sobbing.) *I didn't realize. So all that was going on and we never noticed. . . .*
> *Do any human beings ever realize life while they live it—every, every minute?*
>
> Stage
> Manager: *No. (Pause) The saints and poets, maybe— they do some.*[1]

Emily's observation challenges us to live with awareness, realizing "life while [we] live it—every, every minute." We need to be reminded to appreciate all that is going on around us and inside of us, to be in touch with other people and ourselves, to be mindful of God.

Artists (like the "poets" the Stage Manager mentions) certainly need this kind of awareness to write, or paint, or draw with any authenticity. They need to *pay attention* to what is around them and inside of them. They must take time to penetrate below the surface of things, to rediscover the world with an eye of love, and to "see" into reality. Being an artist involves "grasping life in its depth," as the sensitive artist Vincent Van Gogh once wrote.[2]

But artists are not the only people who must grasp life deeply. Every person can be viewed as a special kind of artist; we are artists of our own lives. If we are to live with any authenticity, we must join those "saints and poets" who grasp life at its depth.

To live so deeply is a special challenge, for it is so easy to be superficial. We are so busy! We have so many urgent things to do, so many people to meet, so many books to read, so many events to attend. Either our jobs demand time and overtime, or we are unemployed and spend much of our time either looking for work or worrying about not finding it. Our families need lots of time and energy. Our studies could fill every working hour. Our houses or apartments or yards beg for our attention. We promise to do things for the church or for community organizations. Problems in many parts of the world concern us, and we are frustrated by not being able to do anything. We simply don't have the time—our calendars are filled with appointments: doctors, dentists, music lessons, potlucks, concerts, sporting events, meetings. . . .

Someday, after driving the children around, or mowing the lawn, or putting in some overtime, or coming in from a ball game, you might fall exhausted in a chair. And maybe, instead of falling asleep, your mind will look over the day with its knocks and opportunities. You may even find some questions lingering around the edges: "What am I doing in all this activity and noise? Where am I going?" Or maybe even that age-old irritator, "Who am I?" If you read poetry, you may remember T. S. Eliot:

> Endless invention, endless experiment,
> Brings knowledge of motion, but not of stillness;
> Knowledge of speech, but not of silence;
> Knowledge of words, and ignorance of the Word. . . .
>
> Where is the Life we have lost in living?
> Where is the wisdom we have lost in knowledge?
> Where is the knowledge we have lost in information?[3]

Perhaps we need to flop into a chair more often—before we are exhausted. We need more leisure time to touch those inner dimensions of our lives, to ask some fundamental questions, or just to be.

> Leisure is not the inevitable result of spare time, a holiday, a weekend or a vacation. It is, in the first place, an attitude of mind, a condition of the soul. . . . Leisure implies . . . an attitude of nonactivity, of inward calm, of silence, it means not being "busy," but letting things happen. Leisure is a form of silence, of that silence which is the prerequisite of the apprehension of reality: only the silent hear and those who do not remain silent do not hear.

> Silence, as it is used in this context, does not mean "dumbness" or "noiselessness"; it means more nearly that the soul's power to "answer" to the reality of the world is left undisturbed. For leisure is a receptive attitude of mind, a contemplative attitude, and it is not only the occasion but also the capacity for steeping oneself in the whole of creation. . . .
>
> Leisure is not the attitude of mind of those who actively intervene, but of those who are open to everything; not of those who grab and grab hold, but of those who leave the reins loose and who are free and easy themselves—almost like someone falling asleep, for one can only fall asleep by "letting oneself go." . . . When we really let our minds rest contemplatively on a rose in bud, on a child at play, on a divine mystery, we are rested and quickened as though by a dreamless sleep. . . . It is in these silent receptive moments that the soul of man is sometimes visited by an awareness of what holds the world together.[4]

Such an attitude pits us against compulsive busyness, against drivenness. It leads toward solitude and contemplation—toward creating an inner receptivity, a space where we can hear our deepest longings, realize what life is about, penetrate into reality. It can mean making a space for God. It is prayer.

Jesus was a very busy person (Mark 6:31), so busy that his friends thought he would go mad (Mark 3:20-21). He was seldom left alone. So he had to make time to be alone, to give undivided attention to God, to pray (Mark 1:35; 6:46-47; 14:32-42; Matt. 14:22-25; 26:36-46; Luke 4:42; 6:12-13; 11:1-2; 22:39-46). Those times must have given him "awareness of what holds the world together," of his own identity, of his mission, and of his relationship with God.

If Jesus needed such solitude for prayer, for listening to God, we certainly do! Martin Luther once said, "I have so much business I cannot get on without spending three hours daily in prayer."[5] I usually do just the opposite: the busier I am, the less I pray. When I was writing the first version of this book, I remember having so much to do that I hardly found time to pray. Many people share and understand that problem. It's the opposite extreme they are suspicious of. If I told you that I had no trouble finding time to pray, that I spent three hours *every day* in prayer, you might wonder if I was very "productive." You might even think I was wasting time, or not earning my pay. What would people think if you did that?

Well, it takes time to stop for contemplation and prayer. It also takes courage.

I went on a weeklong silent retreat. The first night the director of the retreat told us to set up a daily schedule that included five hour-long periods of prayer. I went to my room and began setting up my books, rearranging the furniture. I went to the kitchen to see whether there was anything to eat. I took a nap—anything to avoid making that schedule, to avoid entering silence for prayer.

Gradually I realized that I was afraid. I could hardly pray for fifteen minutes; now I had to pray for five hours! Then I read a text assigned to me, words that Haggai had written for people rebuilding the temple in Jerusalem: "Take heart. . . . Begin the work, for I am with you, says the Lord of Hosts, and my spirit is present among you. Have no fear" (2:4-5, NEB). I needed that.

Since most of what we learn and hear urges us to hustle, chase, and cram, it takes courage to stop for leisure—and especially to stop for prayer. But what's more wasteful—to push hard until we drop, dead tired, or to be quiet and perhaps touch the depth of life? Isaiah seems to speak to us as we rush around:

> *Thus says the Lord God, the Holy One of Israel,*
> *"In returning and rest you shall be saved;*
> *in quietness and in trust shall be your strength."*
> *And you would not, but you said,*
> *"No! We will speed upon our horses"*
> *[or cars or planes—or we will just run the rat race].*
>
> —30:15-16, RSV

"It is hard to leave our people, our job, and the hectic places where we are needed, in order to be with the One from whom all good things come." Yet, once we flop in the chair, we realize we need such a time, such a place for God. And such a time as this "can unmask the illusion of busyness, usefulness, and indispensability. It is a way of being empty and useless in the presence of God and of proclaiming our basic belief that all is grace and nothing is simply the result of hard work."[6]

The world really doesn't need more busy people, maybe not even more intelligent people. It needs "deep people,"[7] people who know that they need

> solitude, if they are going to find out who they are;
> silence, if their words are to mean anything;
> reflection, if their actions are to have any
>   significance;
> contemplation, if they are to see the world as
>   it really is;
> prayer, if they are going to be conscious of God,
>   if they are to "know God and enjoy God forever."

The world needs people who want their lives not only to be filled, but to be full and fulfilled. If we are to be artists of our lives, we need to be in touch with the One who is *"a greater artist than all other artists . . .* [who] made neither statues nor pictures nor books; but loudly proclaimed that he made . . . *living men,* immortals."[8] The world needs people who will allow time for God to recreate them, play with them, touch them as an Artist who is making something beautiful with their lives.

18

This book is for busy people who also want to be deep people. It is a book that explores spirituality, "a way of living in depth."[9] Spirituality has to do with being in touch with our spirit and with the Spirit of God (Rom. 8:14-17; 1 Cor. 2:9-13). It is a way of being awake to the world around us and in us, of making space for God.

This book is about the spiritual life, or about "sanctification," as theologians sometimes call it. It is about living a life for God in our world. More specifically, it is about prayer, prayer which is based on the realization that we belong to God and thus live our lives saying thanks to God. It is meant to encourage you to know God, to enjoy God forever, and in the process, to touch life at some depth. It is concerned to show that such a spirituality and prayerful or contemplative life is not only meant for "saints" but for all God's people, as they go to office or lab, change diapers, fix the car, study, or drive the tractor.

I stayed in a monastery for four days. I went to the seven services of prayer and worship that the monks have each day—beginning at 2:30 A.M. Toward the end of my stay I asked the abbot how I could continue some kind of regular discipline of prayer. I explained that it had been relatively easy to find time for prayer during my stay in the monastery, where it was all structured for me and it was a novelty. But what about when I was back on the job? He said, "The first thing is that you have to want to pray." No amount of discipline or exercise or reading will do it if there is no desire.

This book presupposes that you want to deepen your life and your prayers—and also that you would like to learn some new ways to pray. It was written to help you experience and practice various ways of praying, to discuss them with others, and to expand the possibilities of prayer in your life. You are invited to do the exercises as suggested. Later, as you develop a discipline of prayer, you can discuss and perhaps adapt these exercises to your personal use. If you choose not to do these exercises each day, you will lose the main intent and experience of the course.

You may feel awkward at first doing these spiritual exercises. That's OK. You are still asked to do them, to learn what they involve. Even if you've already found a satisfactory way to pray, you are encouraged to complete these exercises—to expand and enrich what you are already doing.

This course is intended not just for thought and discussion, but for making space in your day for God—for prayer. We usually give God the leftover time of our day. But since there is hardly enough time in a day for all we have to do, there is very little leftover time. I hope you will explore times and ways of being aware of God, of living in God's presence.

Making space for God takes some discipline. At first it may sound like one more thing you "have to do" in your already hassled life. But, as you know, it takes discipline to do anything well, and it is no different with prayer. We make appointments with everyone. Maybe we should make an appointment also with God.

I used to write in my daily calendar "7-7:30 A.M.—Prayer." But many times I passed that up. It was one more thing to pass by that day. Now I write "7-7:30 A.M.—God." Somehow that's a little harder to neglect.

However, by all means be gentle with yourself. We get so down on ourselves when we attempt something and fail to do it or fail in doing it. We can do the same with prayer. We can get down on ourselves, think we are not "doing as well as others," punish ourselves, get more rigidly determined, and want to forget it all. Remember, prayer takes time and practice. So be gentle. And make whatever happens a part of your conversation with God.

Thomas Merton, who spoke from experience, gave a helpful reminder:

In the spiritual life there are no tricks and no short cuts. . . . One cannot begin to face the real difficulties of the life of prayer and meditation unless one is first perfectly content to be a beginner and really experience oneself as one who knows little or nothing, and has a desperate need to learn the bare rudiments. Those who think they "know" from the beginning never, in fact, come to know anything. . . .

We do not want to be beginners. But let us be convinced of the fact that we will never be anything else but beginners, all our life.[10]

Even as I write this book, I realize how much of a beginner I am. I invite you to explore with me some Scripture, some thoughts, some exercises, some readings that I have found useful as I continue to begin a discipline of spirituality and prayer.

* * *

The chapters in this book are all organized in the same way. They begin with my own Reflection on the topic of the chapter. This Reflection is followed by readings, called Windows to Insight, which you can use as a basis for your own daily reflection on the topic. The readings include Scripture, hymns, a saying from the Desert Fathers (people from the third and fourth centuries who went into the Egyptian desert to live a life of silence, solitude, and prayer)[11], and other selections from a variety of writers in a variety of religious traditions.

Any choice of readings will be limited, arbitrary, and very personal. The selections I chose to include in this book are some that have helped me see beyond my own narrow viewpoint. Perhaps you will want to look at the books from which the excerpts came. These writers can be guides who do not ask for imitation, but invite you to search.

These readings are not meant as dogmatic statements or as statements with which you will always agree. If one does not appeal to you, go to another that does. Then stop and reflect on it. You may find yourself coming back to excerpts that you passed over and learning to appreciate them. These selections are meant to stimulate your own reflection and meditation. I hope they become windows through which you view a broad landscape of insights into prayer and the spiritual life.

Following Windows to Insight are some exercises that you are asked to do at home each day and in your group sessions. When the exercises call for a written response, please do your writing in your own journal (any notebook with lots of blank pages will do). The exercises may seem strange at first, but you are encouraged to do them anyway. They will help you experience many different forms of prayer so that by the end of this book (or course), you will be able to choose those that seem most appropriate for you.

Keeping your journal is an important part of this course, not only for recording your answers to various exercises but also for jotting down your personal thoughts, reactions, and prayers. The journal will help you both as an individual and as a member of a class by giving you material for thought and discussion.

The art in this book is not intended simply for illustration. Think of it as another means to stimulate your imagination and reflection, another window to insight. Matthew Fox asks: "Who will support and encourage us on our spiritual . . . way?" And he answers: "Certainly artists will."[12] This has been true for me. Some artists reveal a deep insight into reality, a capacity to see beneath the surface of nature and people, an awareness that uncovers for us a spiritual vitality in our world, in ourselves—and points us toward God. What has struck me is that a truly contemplative and prayerful person seems to have a similar capacity for seeing deeply into reality, the ability to pay attention to what is beneath the surface, a willingness to concentrate long enough to catch a vision.

One of the most important—and most neglected— elements in the beginnings of the interior life is the ability to respond to reality, to see the value and the beauty in ordinary things, to come alive to the splendor that is all around us in the creatures of God.[13]

If that is true, the artists included in this book have been an enormous help in nourishing my interior life. I am especially grateful to Vincent Van Gogh, whom I have known since my ninth-grade teacher took our class to an exhibit of his works at the Chicago Art Institute. In his art Van Gogh was trying to grasp life at its depth.[14] Since I have found that spirituality means living in depth, I believe I have learned something of spirituality from Van Gogh. Perhaps you have a favorite artist who supports and encourages you on your spiritual way—be that artist a painter, poet, musician, sculptor, photographer, calligrapher, or whatever. A person in one of my groups asked, "Do I have to get something out of the pictures? They don't do anything for me." The answer is no. But they are included to show you one more way—alongside Scripture, poetry, music, and readings—that may eventually be a help to you on your spiritual journey and a stimulus to spiritual insight.

The art in this book is an invitation to awareness and contemplation using all the media available to us. An invitation to see beneath the surface of things to the Source and Creator of it all—our almighty, creative, artistic God. God, the artist who

painted the painted desert, the shades of the sea which change with each day, the pastels of the sunset, the black of a stormy night, the silver of a clearly seen Milky Way, the red of blood, the green of the earth, the yellow of grain in ripe fields, the blue of a French Impressionist sky.[15]

We are God's work of art (Eph. 2:10). We are being created and recreated by the saving touch of Christ, who, Van Gogh said, "is more of an artist than the artists," who working in living flesh and living spirit, made living people, instead of statues![16]

We too become artists as we come to know our Creator more intimately.

Each of us becomes the artist as we allow ourselves to be open to the reality of the Other and give expression to that encounter either in words or paint or stone or in the fabric of our lives. Each of us who has come to know and relate to the Other and expresses this in any way is an artist in spite of himself/herself. . . . In the final analysis meditation is the art of living life in its fullest and deepest. Genuine religion and art are two names for the same incredible meeting with reality and give expression to that experience in some manner.[17]

Matthew Fox says it so strongly: "There is no distinction between the artist and the person who has experienced God. No experiencer of God is not an artist."[18]

For these reasons I have included works of a few artists who may open up ways for us to be more aware of life and the creative Source of life.

FOOTNOTES

1. Wilder, *Our Town*, 100.
2. Van Gogh, *The Complete Letters of Vincent Van Gogh*, 197, I, 365.
3. Eliot, "Choruses from 'The Rock,' " *Collected Poems 1909-1935*.
4. Piper, *Leisure, The Basis of Culture*, 40-42.
5. Foster, *The Celebration of Discipline*, 31.
6. Nouwen, *The Living Reminder*, 51-52.
7. Foster, 1.
8. Van Gogh, B8, III, 496.
9. Fox, *Whee, Wee, We—All the Way Home*, I.
10. Merton, *The Climate of Monastic Prayer*, 52-53.
11. I included sayings from the Desert Fathers because I thought it would be interesting and challenging for readers to get to know these early guides in the spiritual life. Some books that have introduced them to me are:
    Ward, *The Sayings of the Desert Fathers*
    Nouwen, *The Way of the Heart*
    Nomura, *Desert Wisdom; Sayings from the Desert Fathers*
    Merton, *The Wisdom of the Desert*
12. Fox, 189.
13. Merton, from *A Thomas Merton Reader*, edited by Thomas P. McDonnell, 386-7.
14. Van Gogh, 197, I, 365.
15. Fox, 82.
16. Van Gogh, B9, III, 499.
17. Kelsey, *The Other Side of Silence, A Guide to Christian Meditation*, 27.
18. Fox, 85.

WINDOWS
TO INSIGHT

*I . . . wrestle with nature long enough for her to tell me
her secret.*

—Vincent Van Gogh, *The Complete Letters*, 393, II, 348

*I do not invent the whole picture;
on the contrary, I find it all ready in nature,
only it must be disentangled.*

—Vincent Van Gogh, *The Complete Letters*, B19, III, 518

*The Fountain
in the Garden of St. Paul's Hospital*

—Vincent Van Gogh

LONGING FOR GOD

Like a deer that yearns
for running streams,
so my soul is yearning
for you, my God.

My soul is thirsting for God,
the God of my life;
when can I enter and see
the face of God?

My tears have become my bread,
by night, by day,
as I hear it said all the day long:
"Where is your God?"

These things will I remember
as I pour out my soul:
how I would lead the rejoicing crowd
into the house of God,
amid cries of gladness and thanksgiving,
the throngs wild with joy.

Why are you cast down, my soul,
why groan within me?
Hope in God; I will still praise the Lord,
my savior and my God.

—Psalm 42:1-5, *A New Translation*

THIRSTING AFTER THE LIVING GOD

Not twenty centuries and more have been able to darken the golden glow of the immortal song that has come to us in the forty-second Psalm . . . in which the home-sickness of our human heart cries after the Source of our life.

What here grips so mightily is the ardent fervor that breathes throughout this whole psalm, the passionate outpouring of soul. . . . In this psalm the heart itself pushes and drives. It is not from without but from the inner chamber of the heart that the home-sickness after the living God irresistibly wells upward. . . .

"My souls pants, yea, thirsts after the living God." Not after a Creed regarding God, not after an idea of God, not after a remembrance of God, not after a Divine Majesty, that, far removed from the soul, stands over against it as a God in words or in phrases, but after God Himself, after God in His holy outpouring of strength and grace, after God Who is alive, Who . . . in holy exhibition of love reveals Himself to you and in you as the living God.

You feel that all learning falls away, all dogma, all formulas, everything that is external and abstract, everything that exhausts itself in words. . . . It is not your idea, not your understanding, not your thinking, not your reasoning, not even your profession of faith, that here can quench the thirst. The home-sickness goes out after God Himself. . . . It is not the Name of God but God Himself Whom your soul desires and can not do without.

—Abraham Kuyper, *To Be Near unto God,* pp. 671-675

Abba Poemen said about Abba Pior that every single day he made a fresh beginning.

—Yushi Nomura, *Desert Wisdom: Sayings from the Desert Fathers*, p. 1

JESUS AT PRAYER

[Jesus] made the disciples get into the boat and go before him to the other side [of the lake], while he dismissed the crowds. And after he had dismissed the crowds, he went up on the mountain by himself to pray. When evening came, he was there alone. . . . And in the fourth watch of the night [between three and six a.m.!] he came to them, walking on the seas.

—Matthew 14:22-25, RSV

That evening after sunset they brought to him all who were ill or possessed by devils; and the whole town was there, gathered at the door. He healed many who suffered from various diseases. . . . Very early next morning he got up and went out. He went away to a lonely spot and remained there in prayer.

—Mark 1:32-35, NEB

TOO "BUSY"

One of the dinner guests, on hearing this, said to him, "Blessed is the one who will eat bread in the kingdom of God!" Then Jesus said to him, "Someone gave a great dinner and invited many. At the time for the dinner he sent his slave to say to those who had been invited, 'Come; for everything is ready now.' But they all alike began to make excuses. The first said to him, 'I have bought a piece of land, and I must go out and see it; please accept my regrets.' Another said, 'I have bought five yoke of oxen, and I am going to try them out; please accept my regrets.' Another said, 'I have just been married, and therefore I cannot come.' So the slave returned and reported this to his master. Then the owner of the house became angry and said to his slave, 'Go out at once into the streets and lanes of the town and bring in the poor, the crippled, the blind, and the lame.' And the slave said, 'Sir, what you ordered has been done, and there is still room.' Then the master said to the slave, 'Go out into the roads and lanes, and compel people to come in, so that my house may be filled. For I tell you, none of those who were invited will taste my dinner.'"

—Luke 14:16-24, NRSV

COVENANT

God
knocks at my door
seeking a home for his son.

Rent is cheap, I say.

I don't want to rent. I want to buy, says God.

I'm not sure I want to sell,
but you might come in to look around.

I think I will, says God.

I might let you have a room or two.

I like it, says God. I'll take the two.
You might decide to give me more some day.
I can wait, says God.

I'd like to give you more,
but it's a bit difficult. I need some space for me.

I know, says God, but I'll wait. I like what I see.

Hm, maybe I can let you have another room.
I really don't need that much.

Thanks, says God, I'll take it. I like what I see.

I'd like to give you the whole house
but I'm not sure . . .

Think on it, says God. I wouldn't put you out.
Your house would be mine and my son would live in it.
You'd have more space that you'd ever had before.

I don't understand at all.

I know, says God, but I can't tell you about that.
You'll have to discover it for yourself.
That can only happen if you let me have the whole house.

A bit risky, I say.

Yes, says God, but try me.

I'm not sure—
I'll let you know.

I can wait, says God. I like what I see.

—Margaret Halaska. This beautiful, unpublished poem
was given to me at a retreat by someone who knew the author.

TAKE TIME TO BE HOLY

Take time to be holy, speak oft with thy Lord;
Abide in Him always, and feed on His Word;
Make friends of God's children, help those who are weak,
Forgetting in nothing His blessing to seek.

Take time to be holy, the world rushes on;
Spend much time in secret with Jesus alone;
By looking to Jesus, like Him thou shalt be;
Thy friends in thy conduct His likeness shall see.

Take time to be holy, let Him be thy Guide,
And run not before Him, whatever betide;
In joy or in sorrow still follow thy Lord,
And looking to Jesus, still trust in His Word.

Take time to be holy, be calm in thy soul;
Each thought and each motive beneath His control;
Thus led by His Spirit to fountains of love,
Thou soon shalt be fitted for service above.

—William D. Longstaff, 1822-1894

PRAYER IS THE SOUL'S SINCERE DESIRE

Prayer is the soul's sincere desire,
Unuttered or expressed,
The motion of a hidden fire
That trembles in the breast.

Prayer is the burden of a sigh,
The falling of a tear,
The upward glancing of the eye,
When none but God is near.

Prayer is the Christian's vital breath,
The Christian's native air,
A watchword at the gates of death;
We enter heaven with prayer.

Prayer is the contrite sinner's voice,
Returning from his ways,
While angels in their songs rejoice
And cry, "Behold, he prays!"

O Thou by whom we come to God,
The life, the truth, the way,
The path of prayer Thyself hast trod:
Lord, teach us how to pray.

—James Montgomery, 1771-1854

THE CONTEMPLATIVE LIFE

The contemplative life is the God-conscious life. It is the life that knows its end and can rest in that knowledge. The Psalmist spoke of it: Be still, and know that I am God. We read of it in Hebrews: There remaineth a rest for the people of God.

John Calvin put it into the first question and answer of his Genevan Catechism. His question was fundamental: What is the chief end of man? And his answer was crystal-clear: To know God and enjoy Him forever. That is the eternal Sabbath which begins here: Delight in the knowledge of God. . . .

The knowledge of God is proper to us as creatures, and it satisfies. That is the finest fruit of the contemplative life: to know and enjoy God. No one will care to ask what such enjoyment is for. It is enough for us. So far from being caught in the web of natural process, snared in the fatality of endless busyness, we can rest in that knowledge.

For man is a creature who can know. . . .

We see that once back there in Paradise. When God had done making the animals, we read this: "And the Lord God formed every beast of the field and every fowl of the air, and brought them unto Adam to see what he would name them." There we have it: a mind to know and to name. The capacity for conscious appreciation. The leisure, the spiritual freedom, to enjoy. Man, conscious reflector of the glory. Homo sapiens, man knowing, not quite submerged in homo faber, man doing. Homo ludens, even, man as artist, man playing. The knowledge of God, which begins in the saving knowledge of Grace through faith, makes for rest and enjoyment. That is the finest fruit of the contemplative life.

Contemplation itself, of course, is not indolence; it is not idle. The saints work hard. Mary's effort at the feet was no easier than Martha's in the kitchen. Gethsemane is unique for its ardor. Jacob wrestled in prayer. Contemplation represents not an escape from drudgery into entertainment, but the positive education of leisure. Some people are too lazy to engage in it, too bored to be still. It embarrasses them, the confrontation in solitude of self, and God, and destiny. Robert Louis Stevenson, perhaps with tongue in cheek, once wrote this of such persons: "There is a sort of dead-alive . . . people about, who are scarcely conscious of living except in the exercise of some conventional occupation. . . . They have dwarfed and narrowed their soul by a life of all work, until here they are at forty, with a listless attention, a mind vacant of all material for amusement, and not one thought to rub against another while waiting for the train."

In its deeper levels this of Stevenson is a kind of boredom too, a boredom springing from neglect of the contemplative life. For boredom also is an earmark of life in our day. The poets have seen it and are good reporters. "Ennui, ennui, ennui," says Christopher Fry in a recent drama, and he toasts the vanity of a purposeless life with a yawn. It had been Oscar Wilde's final dread. "The only horrible thing," he had said, "the only horrible thing in the world is ennui." It is horrible, of course. When we cannot find God, we cannot find his world and his wonders. Or finding these, we can only use and exploit them; we cannot appreciate and enjoy them.

—Henry Zylstra, *The Testament of Vision,* pp. 185, 187,188

PERSEVERANCE IN PRAYER

Lifting up our hearts,
We should ever aspire to God
And pray without ceasing.
Still, such is our weakness
It must be supported by many helps,
Such our sluggishness
It needs to be goaded.
Consequently fitting it is
That each one of us should set apart
Certain hours for this exercise,
Hours that should not pass without prayer,
Hours when all the heart's devotion
Should completely engage in prayer.

When should we pray?
Upon arising in the morning,
Before we begin daily work,
When we sit down to a meal,
When by God's blessing we have eaten,
When we are preparing to retire.

No superstitious observance of hours, this,
Whereby, as if paying our debt to God,
We fancy ourselves paid up
For the remaining hours.
No, it must be a tutelage for our weakness,
Exercised and repeatedly stimulated.
Whenever we are pressed
Or see others pressed
By any adversity,
Let us hasten back to God,
Not with swift feet
But with eager hearts;
On the other hand,
Let us not permit the prosperity
Of ourselves or others to go unnoticed,
Failing to testify, by praise and thanksgiving,
That we discern God's hand therein.

—John Calvin, *The Piety of John Calvin* by Ford Lewis Battles, pp. 111-112

A child in the cradle, if you watch it at leisure, has the infinite in its eyes.

—Vincent Van Gogh, *The Complete Letters*, 518, III, 2

If one feels the need of something grand, something infinite, something that makes one feel aware of God, one need not go far to find it. I think I see something deeper, more infinite, more eternal than the ocean in the expression of the eyes of a little baby when it wakes in the morning, and coos or laughs because it sees the sun shining on its cradle.

—Vincent Van Gogh, *The Complete Letters*, 242, I, 483

Girl Kneeling in Front of a Cradle

—Vincent Van Gogh

31

EXERCISES

In Session

Reflect on your experience. Is it easy or hard for you to find time to pray, to make space for God in your life? Write down some things that keep you from prayer or from pursuing your spiritual life. Are there thoughts, ideas, attitudes, feelings that might keep you from spending time with God? Are there any ideas that could be reexamined, any attitudes that could be changed, any activities that could be shifted, any priorities that could be rearranged so you would be able to make some time and space for God each day?

At Home

1. Set aside ten to fifteen minutes each day this week to read and reflect on chapter 1. The first day read Reflection; the other days read Windows to Insight. Spend some of the time thinking about what you read. You are also encouraged to jot down your personal reactions and insights in your journal.

    Since you will be doing this kind of reading and reflecting throughout the course, please try to decide when you can make this ten to fifteen minutes available each day. If possible, also decide where you'll be doing your reading and reflecting.

2. Beginning next week, after the second session, you'll be asked to set aside five minutes each day for morning prayers. This week, try to decide on a time for your morning prayers (generally, the closer to the beginning of the day, the better). Also, try to decide on the place for your morning prayers. Record your decision in your journal. Please bring this book and your journal to the next session.

CHAPTER 2

I BELONG

In a picture, I want to say something comforting, as music is comforting. I want to paint men and women with that something of the eternal which the halo used to symbolize. . . .

—Vincent Van Gogh, *The Complete Letters*, 531, III, 25

What is your only comfort in life and in death?

That I am not my own,
but belong—
*   body and soul,*
*   in life and in death—*
to my faithful Savior Jesus Christ.

—Heidelberg Catechism Q & A 1

Sien with Child on Her Lap

—Vincent Van Gogh

REFLECTION

I was speaking at a religious service in a nursing home. I wanted to present something comforting to the aging patients. So I began by saying, "You belong." I was about to continue when a ninety-year-old woman sitting near me in a wheelchair startled me by shouting in her high wheezy voice with both distress and longing, "TO WHOM?"

"You belong."

"To whom?" That is my question at times when I feel alone, isolated, lonely. It's a question many people ask. "Loneliness is one of the most universal human experiences . . . "[1] and is among the worst of human sufferings.

Of course, you do belong somewhere. You belong to a family where at least some people care.

> *Home is the place where, when you have to go there, they have to take you.*[2]

Perhaps you have friends with whom you share some understanding, solidarity, intimacy, and warmth. Or you may belong to a neighborhood, a company, a club, a group, a school, or a church that gives you some sense of identity.

But there may be times when no matter what you do, your family seems distant. None of your friends seem to like you. Nobody calls you on the phone. You get ignored at school, in your church, at your club. No one seems to care what you do or who you are. You're a nobody! You realize how much your identity depends on other people: how they praise you, respect you, react to you, like you—or even dislike you. You feel isolated.

I went to an opening gathering at the divinity school where I was to study for a year. I knew hardly anyone. As we ate ice cream, a few students said hello. A few even chatted for several minutes— until they spotted someone else, someone they knew. The one person I knew was occupied. So I went home—to an empty house. My wife and daughter had not arrived yet. I was all alone in a strange place. I didn't seem to belong.

Most of us know that feeling of being alone, isolated. It's not the same as choosing to be alone once in a while, or being independent at times. It's the feeling that no one is near, that no one remembers, that "no one cares for my soul" (Ps. 142:4), that there is no one to live for. It's a feeling of deep isolation, of not belonging to anyone. And when we have that feeling, "To whom?" becomes our lonely cry of distress and longing.

God hears that question. So what we do at such times is very important for our spiritual as well as for our emotional lives. We can try to escape the loneliness by working harder, even putting in overtime; by reading a book; by going to a bar and joining other lonely people sitting in a row; by playing tennis; by calling someone—anyone. Or we can stay with that loneliness a little while and become aware of life at a deeper level. If we do, we might realize that no amount of work, busyness, food or drink, even of companionship will completely release us from our lonely condition. Something larger, deeper, more lasting is necessary.

If we are quiet long enough to let our faith speak at such times, we might hear a basic truth expressed by St. Paul:

> For no one of us lives, and equally no one of us dies, for himself alone. If we live, we live for the Lord; and if we die, we die for the Lord. Whether therefore we live or die, we belong to the Lord.
>
> —Romans 14:7-8, NEB

Even when events and people say: "You don't belong," God's gentle voice reassures us: "You do belong—to me." "To whom?" is a cry God can both hear and answer. In fact, God is waiting to answer, as a loving parent waits with open arms for a child who has left home.

The parable of the prodigal son tells us, "There is a homecoming for us all because there is a home"![3] Belonging means we have an address, a place where we are "at home." We belong to God and God will not let us go as others might. That belonging is more lasting, more constant, more loving than any belonging that job, school, club, church, friends, or even family can provide. "He made us, we belong to him" (Ps. 100:3, *A New Translation*). We are as precious to God as a portrait is to the artist who painted it, or as a child to the mother who bore it.

> Can a woman forget the infant at her breast, or a loving mother the child of her womb? Even these forget, yet I will not forget you. . . . I have engraved them on the palms of my hands.
>
> —Isaiah 49:15-16, NEB

I have known for a long time that I belong to God. But it came home more poignantly and personally at a week-long silent retreat I attended in Connecticut, a retreat led by a Jesuit priest. I struggled during the week with my relationship to people and to God. I had times of joy and times of confusion, fear, and trouble.

At the end of the week I was given the story of the Annunciation to Mary (Luke 1:26-38) to contemplate. After reading the passage, I was to imagine myself as Mary in her awesome situation.

It was comforting to hear the words: "The Lord be with you." And, when deeply perturbed and full of wonder at the angel's message, to hear: "Do not be afraid; God loves you dearly." To say Mary's response to it all was deeply moving: "I belong to the Lord, body and soul, let it happen as you say" (J. B. Phillips).

Mary knew the Heidelberg Catechism! At least her words brought back to me, with power and depth, words of a catechism I had learned as a child and have known ever since. But now I learned them in a profoundly personal way.

Perhaps you know the opening lines of this Reformation catechism:

> *What is your only comfort in life and in death?*
>
> *That I am not my own*
> *but* belong—
>   *body and soul,*
>   *in life and in death—*
> *to my faithful Savior Jesus Christ.*
>
> —Heidelberg Catechism, Q & A 1

That answer is like a warm shower after being out on a cold day; like an embrace after a time of loneliness; like the hug of a loving parent for a wayward child. It is the covenantal hug of God! It is like hearing the encouraging words of Isaiah 43 as though they were spoken to us personally:

Thus says the LORD,
> *he who created you, O (fill in your name),*
> *he who formed you, O (fill in your name):*

Do not fear, for I have redeemed you;
> *I have called you by name, you are mine.*

—Isaiah 43:1, NRSV (cf. vv. 2-5)

Henri Nouwen wrote in *The Life of the Beloved* that being beloved of God is the core truth about our humanity, and when we are blessed with that deep truth, we can walk through life with a sense of well-being and true belonging (pp. 28, 60).

When we experience belonging to God, we know what salvation means, we are experiencing the *covenant* between God and humanity. The covenant initiates us into an intimate relationship with God. It restores the paradisal companionship God meant for us right from the beginning. In the covenant God pledges: "I will be your God. You shall be my people" (Jer. 31:33; cf. also Gen. 17:7-8)—no matter what! This *gracious* promise of God, first given to Abraham and Sarah, will continue forever (Gen. 17:7).

The life, death, and resurrection of Jesus Christ make this covenant relationship even more concrete and visible to us. In Christ, God addresses us with promises. God makes space for us. We are united with Christ (Col. 2:6). We have put on Christ (Gal. 3:27). We are in Christ. We have been ingrafted into Christ. Christ is the vine and we are the branches (John 15:1-9). In Christ, it is possible for us to live a life of total connectedness with God. "You belong to Christ, and Christ to God" (1 Cor. 3:23, NEB). In the covenant, promised through Sarah and Abraham to all their descendants and renewed by Jesus Christ, realized and celebrated in the church, the body of Christ, we can have the comforting confidence to say: "I am convinced that there is nothing . . . that can separate us from the love of God in Christ Jesus our Lord" (Rom. 8:38-39, NEB). We are addressed by God, and we have an address, a place, with God.

That means we are never isolated. We live constantly in the gracious covenantal presence of God. Knowing that does not solve all our problems, but it can give us a perspective on loneliness. It can help us understand that we do not have to be greedy for attention as a solution to loneliness, we do not have to cling to people for our identity. We get our identity from God. Once we understand that, we should also understand that we no longer have to avoid being alone. In fact, we might want to *look* for times to be alone so we can be with God, so that we can create a space to be aware of our relationship with God, so that we can be reminded that God makes a space for us and that we live continuously in God's gracious presence. We may be able slowly to convert our aloneness from a depressing loneliness into a deep solitude: a precious, fearless space where we are aware that we belong to God.

This sense of belonging is the beginning of any understanding and experience of spirituality and prayer.

FOOTNOTES
1. Nouwen, *Reaching Out*, 14.
2. Frost, "Death of a Hired Man," *Robert Frost's Poems*, 165.
3. Thielicke, *The Waiting Father*, 29.

WINDOWS
TO INSIGHT

[Rembrandt] gives us one work which sums up his entire pilgrimage: The Return of the Prodigal Son. *This son, who delivers himself into his father's hands, surrenders himself to his verdict, is no figure from a parable. But he is Rembrandt himself, he is man, at all times and in all places, who seeks and finds his father's open arms.*

—W. A. Visser 't Hooft, *Rembrandt and the Gospel*, p. 17

The Return of the Prodigal Son

—Rembrandt

THE PARABLE OF THE WAITING PARENT

There was once a man who had two sons; and the younger said to his father, "Father, give me my share of the property." So he divided his estate between them.

A few days later the younger son turned the whole of his share into cash and left home for a distant country, where he squandered it in reckless living. He had spent it all, when a severe famine fell upon that country and he began to feel the pinch. So he went and attached himself to one of the local landowners, who sent him on to his farm to mind the pigs. He would have been glad to fill his belly with the pods that the pigs were eating; but no one gave him anything.

Then he came to his senses and said, "How many of my father's paid servants have more food than they can eat, and here am I, starving to death! I will set off and go to my father, and say to him, 'Father, I have sinned, against God and against you; I am no longer fit to be called your son; treat me as one of your paid servants.'"

So he set out for his father's house.

But while he was still a long way off his father saw him, and his heart went out to him. He ran to meet him, flung his arms round him, and kissed him. The son said, "Father, I have sinned, against God and against you; I am no longer fit to be called your son." But the father said to his servants, "Quick! fetch a robe, my best one, and put it on him; put a ring on his finger and shoes on his feet. Bring the fatted calf and kill it, and let us have a feast to celebrate the day. For this son of mine was dead and has come back to life; he was lost and is found."

And the festivities began.

—Luke 15:11-24 (NEB)

A parable of abundant fatherly compassion:
A son had estranged himself from his father,
Had dissolutely wasted his substance,
Had grievously offended against him.
Yet the father embraces him with open arms,
Does not wait for him to ask for pardon,
But anticipates him,
Afar off recognizes him returning,
Runs willingly to meet him,
Comforts him,
Receives him into favor.
Great though this human compassion is,
He teaches us a greater.
No mere father He, but the best
And kindest Father of all He is to us—
Provided we cast ourselves,
Ungrateful, rebellious, forward children
Though we are,
Upon His mercy.

—John Calvin, *The Piety of John Calvin* by Ford Lewis Battles, p. 102

TO THE LORD
PSALM 100

Shout to the Lord, all the land;
Serve the Lord with joy;
Come before God with laughter.
Know that the Lord is God;
We belong to the Lord our maker,
To God, who tends us like sheep.
Come to God's gates with thanks;
Come to God's court with praise;
Praise and bless the Lord's name.
Truly the Lord is good;
God is always gracious,
And faithful age after age.

—*The Psalms: A New Translation for Prayer and Worship,* translated by
Gary Chamberlain, ©1984, The Upper Room. Used by permission.

No one of us lives,
and equally no one of us dies,
for himself alone.
If we live, we live for the Lord;
and if we die, we die for the Lord.
Whether therefore we live or die, we belong to the Lord.

—Romans 14:7-8, NEB

Everything belongs to you . . .
yet you belong to Christ, and Christ to God.

—1 Corinthians 3:21-23, NEB

NEARER, STILL NEARER

Nearer, still nearer, close to Thy heart,
Draw me, my Savior, so precious Thou art.
Fold me, O fold me close to Thy breast;
Shelter me safe in that haven of rest.

Nearer, still nearer, nothing I bring,
Naught as an offering to Jesus my King—
Only my sinful, now contrite heart;
Grant me the cleansing Thy blood doth impart.

Nearer, still nearer, Lord, to be Thine,
Sin with its follies I gladly resign,
All of its pleasures, pomp and its pride;
Give me but Jesus, my Lord crucified.

Nearer, still nearer, while life shall last,
Till safe in glory my anchor is cast;
Through endless ages, ever to be
Nearer, my Savior, still nearer to Thee.

—Mrs. C. H. Morris, 1862-1929

LONELINESS

It is this most basic human loneliness that threatens us and is so hard to face. Too often we will do everything possible to avoid the confrontation with the experience of being alone, and sometimes we are able to create the most ingenious devices to prevent ourselves from being reminded of this condition. Our culture has become most sophisticated in the avoidance of pain, not only our physical pain but our emotional and mental pain as well. . . . We have become so used to this state of anesthesia, that we panic when there is nothing or nobody left to distract us. When we have no project to finish, no friend to visit, no book to read, no television to watch or no record to play, and when we are left all alone by ourselves we are brought so close to the revelation of our basic human aloneness and are so afraid of experiencing an all-pervasive sense of loneliness that we will do anything to get busy again and continue the game which makes us believe that everything is fine after all. . . .

When our loneliness drives us away from ourselves into the arms of our companions in life, we are, in fact, driving ourselves into excruciating relationships, tiring friendships and suffocating embraces. To wait for moments or places where no pain exists, no separation is felt and where all human restlessness has turned into inner peace is waiting for a dreamworld. No friend or lover, no husband or wife, no community or commune will be able to put to rest our deepest cravings for unity and wholeness.

—Henri Nouwen, *Reaching Out*, pp. 16, 17, 19

INFINITY

What else is there that I can tell You about Yourself, except that You are the One without whom I cannot exist, the Eternal God from whom alone I, a creature of time, can draw the strength to live, the Infinity who gives meaning to finiteness? And when I tell You all this, then I have given myself my true name, the name I ever repeat when I pray in David's Psalter, "Tuus sum ego." I am the one who belongs not to himself, but to You. I know no more than this about myself, nor about You, O God of my life, Infinity of my finiteness.

What a poor creature You have made me, O God! All I know about You and about myself is that you are the eternal mystery of my life. Lord, what a frightful puzzle humankind is! We belong to You, and You are the Incomprehensible—incomprehensible in Your Being, and even more so in Your ways and judgments. . . .

But if You were not incomprehensible, You would be inferior to me, for my mind could grasp and assimilate You. You would belong to me, instead of I to You. And that would truly be hell, if I should belong only to myself! It would be the fate of the damned, to be doomed to pace up and down for all eternity in the cramped and confining prison of my own finiteness.

—Karl Rahner, *Encounters with Silence*, pp. 7-8

SALVATION AS BELONGING

The message of Jesus is about God as the one who is towards us, who speaks to us, to whom we belong. To experience that mutual belonging is salvation. In that experience God's saving power is made manifest. In contemporary terms, salvation means belonging. The way we experience the opposite of salvation is alienation.

Belonging and alienation are words that speak to us today. We know what alienation is on the personal level, on the social level, and on the religious level. Alienation means our utmost misery. The opposite of alienation is belonging. Translated into our terms today, the message of Jesus is: You belong! You don't have to earn it, this ultimate belonging. It is a given fact. It's the most basic truth of your life. Don't you know that in your heart of hearts? Jesus asks us. And Paul will say the same thing in his own words: "By grace you have been saved." You belong. You are members of the family, no longer alien. Now act accordingly. Act as one acts when one belongs.

God's gift of belonging has implications towards yourself, towards others, towards society. The kingdom of God has, all of a sudden, social implications.

So Jesus comes and proclaims the kingdom of God with power available to anyone here and now. We merely need to accept the gift of belonging. That is conversion.

Accept your belonging, Jesus says. Snap out of your alienation. Don't hang on to your private little self. Open yourself to the gift of belonging. All the joy of heaven is yours for the taking—no, for the giving of yourself. That is God's kingdom and conversion. That is what Jesus preached.

—Brother David Steindl-Rast, "Who Is Jesus Christ for Us Today?"
Chapter 3 in *The Christ and the Bodhisattva*, pp. 103-104

Abba Mios was asked by a soldier whether God would forgive a sinner. After instructing him at some length, the old man asked him: Tell me, my dear, if your cloak were torn, would you throw it away? Oh, no! he replied, I would mend it and wear it again. The old man said to him: Well, if you care for your cloak, will not God show mercy to his own creature?

—Yushi Nomura, *Desert Wisdom: Sayings from the Desert Fathers*, p. 11

THE SOULS WHICH I HAVE MADE

There is subtle charm about the thing that we have made, and this is by no means always because of its intrinsic value, but rather because we have made it ourselves.

He who has studied portrait painting and for the sake of perfecting himself in his art copies celebrated originals, puts a value on his copy, which, in his estimation, the far more beautiful original does not possess. . . .

A contributor to a monthly or quarterly periodical deems his own article, when it comes out, the best of that number. This holds good in every department of life. There is no end of interest in produce that we ourselves have raised. Cattle bred on our own stock farm are preferred to any other. We are more happy in a house that we ourselves have built. . . .

And yet though too much self-complacency may play a part in this, this is not the principal trait that dominates the preference that is given to a product of one's own.

This is felt at once when you reckon with mother-joy which revels in play with her own child in a way that no woman can in play with the child of another.

Truly, self-delusion and selfishness play all too frequently anything but a subordinate part in this joy of the mother-heart over her own child; but history of all ages, and folklore of all lands bear witness, that an altogether different string from that of selfishness vibrates in this wealth of mother-love, and that the music peculiar to this other string is only understood when the sacred fact is brought to mind that it is she who bore the child.

In her own child the mother sees, and is conscious of, a part of her own life. The child does not stand by the side of the mother as number one alongside of number two, but in the child the mother-life is extended.

This selfsame trait asserts itself in every product of our own, whether it be our own thought, knowledge, exertion, will-power or perseverance; . . . there is always something in it of our own, a distinctive something that we imprint upon it, an individual stamp that we have put upon it, something that makes us feel about it as we can never feel about anything that we ourselves have not made.

And by this trait of our human heart God comforts the sinner. That trait is in us because it is in God. And of this trait God says that it operates in the Divine Father-heart for our good, because where there is a soul at stake, God can never forget that He Himself has made it.

"For I will not contend forever, neither will I be always wroth; for the spirit should fail before me, and the souls which I have made" (Isa. lvii, 16).

As little as a mother can allow her just anger with the child of her own bosom to work itself out to the end, just so little can God's displeasure with a soul exhaust itself, because He Himself *has made it.*

"As a father pitieth his children, so the Lord pitieth them that fear Him" (Ps. 103, 13). "Though a mother may forget her sucking child, yet will I not forget thee" (Isa. xlix, 15).

The Father-name of God expresses completely this selfsame richly comforting thought. . . .

That you have been created after God's Image, declares that by virtue of your creation, God feels Himself related to you. . . .

Because God has made your soul, there is something in it of God Himself, a Divine stamp has been impressed upon you; there is something of God's power, thought, and creative genius in you, as in no other. You are one of the Lord's own works of art, precisely like which He created none other. . . .

An artist who had a collection of his paintings on exhibition in a museum, and discovered one day that one of his pictures was gone, could not rest until it had been traced and restored to its place on the wall.

So does God miss every soul that falls away from Him, because it is a soul that He has made; and what Jesus described in such touching and beautiful terms in the parables of the lost penny, the lost sheep, and the prodigal son, was born in His heart from the one thought, that God can not let go the work of His hands, and therefore can not unconcernedly leave the souls of sinners as the prey of perdition, because they are His handiwork, and because He Himself has made them.

—Abraham Kuyper, *To Be Near unto God*, pp. 27-30

PRAYER OF THE HEART

The Way of the Pilgrim is a little book that is highly valued in Russian Orthodox mysticism. It comes from the middle of the nineteenth century. Written in the first person, the book presents itself as the spiritual autobiography of a Russian peasant. It shows that "mental prayer" can be practiced not only in a monastic cell but by a layperson even under the peculiar conditions of a wandering life. The prayer taught here is sometimes called the "Jesus Prayer," or the "Prayer of the Heart."

By the grace of God I am a Christian, by my deeds a great sinner, and by calling a homeless rover of the lowest status in life. My possessions comprise but some rusk in a knapsack on my back, and the Holy Bible on my bosom. That is all.

On the twenty-fourth Sunday after Pentecost, I went to church to hear Mass. The first Epistle of St. Paul to the Thessalonians was read. In it we are exhorted, among other things, to pray incessantly, and these words engraved themselves upon my mind. I began to ponder whether it is possible to pray without ceasing, since people must occupy themselves with other things needed for their support.

"What am I to do?" I mused. "Where will I be able to find someone who can explain it to me? I shall go to the churches known for their famous preachers; perhaps there I shall hear something that will enlighten me." And I went.

[He heard a lot of sermons on prayer in general, but did not learn how it was to be done. So he gave up going to church and decided to look for someone who could explain the meaning of unceasing prayer. After much searching he found an elderly man who gave him an answer.]

As we entered his [monastic] cell he said: "The constant inner prayer of Jesus is an unbroken, perpetual calling upon the Divine Name of Jesus with the lips, the mind and the heart, while picturing His lasting presence in one's imagination and imploring His grace wherever one is, in whatever one does, even while one sleeps. This prayer consists of the following words: 'Lord Jesus Christ, have mercy on me!' Those who use this prayer constantly are so greatly comforted that they are moved to say it at all times, for they can no longer live without it. And the prayer will keep on ringing in their hearts of its own accord. Now, do you understand what incessant prayer is?"

"Yes, I do, Father. In the Name of God explain to me how to achieve the mastery of it," I said, feeling overwhelmed with joy.

. . . "Take a seat in solitude and silence. Bend your head, close your eyes, and breathing softly, in your imagination, look into your own heart. Let your mind, or rather, your thoughts, flow from your head down to your heart and say, while breathing: 'Lord Jesus Christ, have mercy on me.' Whisper these words gently, or say them in your mind. Discard all other thoughts. Be serene, persevering and repeat them over and over again."

[He was urged to say the "prayer of the heart" 3,000 times a day; then 6,000 times a day; and later 12,000 times a day. Which, he said, "wearied me to a certain extent; my tongue was somewhat numbed and my jaws still. My palate, too, hurt a little!" But soon "my lips and my tongue recited the words without any effort on my part. I spent the whole day experiencing great happiness."]

I began to feel that the Prayer had, so to speak, passed to my heart. In other words I felt that my heart in its natural beating began, as it were, to utter the words of the Prayer. No longer did I say the Prayer with my lips, but listened attentively to the words formed in my heart, remembering what my now departed elder told me about this state of bliss.

—from *A Treasury of Russian Spirituality*, edited by G. P. Fedotov.
This is only an excerpt, pp. 283-295, from the longer story, pp. 283-345.

SOLITUDE OF HEART

The word solitude can be misleading. It suggests being alone by yourself in an isolated place. When we think about solitaries, our mind easily evokes images of monks or hermits who live in remote places secluded from the noise of the busy world. In fact, the words solitude *and* solitary *are derived from the Latin word* solus, *which means alone, and during the ages many men and women who wanted to live a spiritual life withdrew to remote places—deserts, mountains or deep forests—to live the life of a recluse.*

It is probably difficult, if not impossible, to move from loneliness to solitude without any form of withdrawal from a distracting world, and therefore it is understandable that those who seriously try to develop their spiritual life are attracted to places and situations where they can be alone, sometimes for a limited period of time, sometimes more or less permanently. But the solitude that really counts is the solitude of heart; it is an inner quality or attitude that does not depend on physical isolation. On occasion this isolation is necessary to develop this solitude of heart, but it would be sad if we considered this essential aspect of the spiritual life as a privilege of monks and hermits. It seems more important than ever to stress that solitude is one of the human capacities that can exist, be maintained and developed in the center of a big city, in the middle of a large crowd and in the context of a very active and produc-tive life. A man or woman who has developed this solitude of heart is no longer pulled apart by the most divergent stimuli of the surrounding world but is able to perceive and understand this world from a quiet inner center.

By attentive living we can learn the difference between being present in loneliness and being present in solitude. When you are alone in an office, a house or an empty waiting room, you can suffer from restless loneliness but also enjoy a quiet solitude. When you are teaching in a classroom, listening to a lecture, watching a movie or chatting at a "happy hour," you can have the unhappy feeling of loneliness but also the deep contentment of someone who speaks, listens and watches from the tranquil center of your solitude. It is not too difficult to distinguish between the restless and the restful, between the driven and the free, between the lonely and the solitary in our surroundings. When we live with a solitude of heart, we can listen with attention to the words and the worlds of others, but when we are driven by loneliness, we tend to select just those remarks and events that bring immediate satisfaction to our own craving needs.

—Henri Nouwen, *Reaching Out*, pp. 25-26

A PARABLE OF PRAYER

A father and his son, travelling together in a wagon,
  came to the edge of a forest.
Some bushes, thick with berries,
  caught the child's eye.
"Father," he asked, "may we stop a while
  so that I can pick some berries?"
The father was anxious to complete his journey,
  but he did not have it in his heart
  to refuse the boy's request.
The wagon was called to a halt,
  and the son alighted to pick the berries.

After a while,
  the father wanted to continue on his way.
But his son had become so engrossed in berry-picking
  that he could not bring himself to leave the forest.
"Son!" cried the father, "we cannot stay here all day!
  We must continue our journey!"

Even the father's pleas were not enough
  to lure the boy away.
What could the father do?
Surely he loved his son
  no less for acting so childishly.
He would not think of leaving him behind—
  but he really did have to get going on his journey.

Finally he called out:
  "You may pick your berries for a while longer,
  but be sure you are still able to find me,
  for I shall start moving slowly along the road,
As you work, call out 'Father! Father!'
  every few minutes, and I shall answer you.
As long as you can hear my voice,
  know that I am still nearby.
But as soon as you can no longer hear my answer,
  know that you are lost,
  and run with all your strength to find me!"

—*Your Word Is Fire: The Hasidic Masters on Contemplative Prayer*, edited and
translated by Arthur Green and Barry W. Holtz, pp. 109-110

EXERCISES

In Session

Contemplate the story of the prodigal son (the waiting parent):

1. Read the story in Luke 15:11-24. (Windows, p. 40)
2. Spend fifteen minutes in silence imagining yourself as the son or daughter who is leaving home. Why are you leaving home? What is it like to be away? What happened when you were away? Why did you come back? What is it like to be greeted by a loving parent; to have a banquet thrown for you? These and other such questions can guide your imagination, but don't feel you have to "answer" each question.

    (This is not an exegetical exercise in which you try to "understand" the text. That too is important, but not for this exercise. This exercise is meant to have you "experience" the text as though it were happening to you and then reflect on the text out of your own experience.)
3. End this meditation by repeating for two minutes, very slowly: "I belong to God."
4. Write a prayer (in your journal) on the basis of your experience (5 minutes).

At Home

1. *Morning Prayers*

    Begin each morning by setting aside five minutes. During that time repeat slowly, again and again, "I belong to God." Or, if you want to make this more personal, say: "I belong to you, O God." At first say the words out loud. Then gradually "say" them quietly in your mind and heart.
2. *During the Day*

    Take ten minutes to read and reflect on the textbook materials. On the first day, read the Reflection for chapter 2, "I Belong." On other days use Windows to Insight for your reflections. Record reactions in your journal.
3. About halfway through the week repeat the contemplation of the story of the waiting parent. (See In Session above.)

3

CHAPTER 3

GRATITUDE TAKES NOTHING FOR GRANTED

Gratitude takes nothing for granted, is never unresponsive, is constantly awakening to new wonder, and to praise of the goodness of God.

—Thomas Merton, *Thoughts in Solitude*, p. 42

All nature seems to speak. . . . As for me, I cannot understand why everybody does not see it or feel it; nature or God does it for everyone who has eyes and ears and a heart to understand.

—Vincent Van Gogh, *The Complete Letters*, 248, I, 495

What do you understand by the providence of God?

Providence is
*   the almighty and ever present power of God*
*   by which he upholds, as with his hand,*
*   heaven*
*   and earth*
*   and all creatures,*
*   and so rules them that*
*   leaf and blade,*
*   rain and drought,*
*   fruitful and lean years,*
*   food and drink,*
*   health and sickness,*
*   prosperity and poverty—*
*   all things, in fact, come to us*
*   not by chance*
*   but from his fatherly hand.*

—Heidelberg Catechism, Q & A 27

Cypresses with Two Women

—Vincent Van Gogh

53

REFLECTION

As I was driving around Chicago with my parents, we passed the hospital where I was born. I said to my mother:

"Tell me once again, how was that when I was born—how did you almost die?"

She replied:

"Oh, it wasn't I who almost died. It was you."

Well! Somehow I had twisted the story around all those years.

I've thought about that conversation a lot during the past years. It's helped me realize that my life is a gift. Of course, I had thought that before—that life is a gift. But it comes home to me with particular poignancy when I say to myself:

"On July 3, 1934, I almost died!"

I now accept each day of my life as a gift—a gift for which I am deeply grateful. Life was something that I took for granted so often. But now each day I awake I can say with Hezekiah:

The living, the living, give you thanks O God, as I do today (Isa. 38:19, *New American Bible*).

Gratitude takes nothing for granted. It acknowledges each favor, each gift—both big and small. It also *recognizes the giver*—the relative who shows her love by giving you a gift; the friend who remembers to call you; the person who gives you a compliment or goes out of his way to invite you to go for a walk on a beautiful fall day; the spouse or friend who brings you a cup of coffee when you're exhausted, cooks you a fine dinner, or throws a party for you.

These gifts, and many more like them, seldom leave us cold. They create a momentary surge in us, a slight impulse of recognition—a gift! And at the moment recognition dawns, thankfulness stirs spontaneously in us.

Sometimes our gratitude is a deeper surge of thankful feeling. On that walk among the leaves—the browns and reds and yellows—we stop. We become aware that we are part of something much larger than ourselves. We feel the urge to say "Wow!" or "Isn't this terrific!" or "Thanks!" A Japanese Zen Master put it this way:

> *People often ask me how Buddhists answer the question: "Does God exist?"*
>
> *The other day I was walking along the river. The wind was blowing. Suddenly I thought, Oh! the air really exists. We know that the air is there, but unless the wind blows against our face, we are not aware of it. Here in the wind I was suddenly aware, yes, it's really there.*
>
> *And the sun too. I was suddenly aware of the sun, shining through the bare trees. Its warmth, its brightness, and all this completely free, completely gratuitous. Simply there for us to enjoy.*

> *And without my knowing it, completely sponta-*
> *neously, my two hands came together, and I realized that I*
> *was making a gassho.* And it occurred to me that this is*
> *all that matters: that we can bow, take a deep bow. Just*
> *that. Just that.[1]*

*"Gassho—the gesture of raising the hands palm to palm to indicate respect, gratitude, or humility, or all three" (from *The Three Pillars of Zen*, p. 331).

This Buddhist bow of gratitude toward the Source of all creation can deepen into a Christian kneeling in thanks to the Giver of all good gifts.

Perhaps you've felt that thankful surge that comes from appreciating that you are surrounded by a profusion of gifts. But perhaps not. Not much in our society stimulates us to such appreciation. Instead of suggesting that we give thanks, TV advertising encourages us to be greedy for more gifts. Periodicals tell us of the many things we could own but don't. And our neighbors describe their latest purchases in detail. If we listen to all these voices, we won't feel much gratitude. Instead we'll start thinking that we have practically nothing and need to get more . . . and more.

It's that attitude that makes us hostile—that leads us to guard what we have from others. We need special locks on our doors; we need guns and even bombs to protect it all. We are afraid to share our personal or national resources because much of what we hear says we don't have enough. It looks past what we have to what we do not have and urges us to grab for more.

Greed grabs. Gratitude receives. That's why gratitude often seems like a radical reaction to life. Gratitude takes nothing for granted. When you are truly grateful, you recognize not only the dinner someone prepared as a gift, but also become aware of the person who prepared it. You are cognizant of the concern it took for someone to call, to send a card, to give a compliment. You are aware of the love involved in a routine offer to do the dishes, fix a leaky faucet, take out the garbage. You may get a glimpse at the wonder of friends and family. Maybe you are

> *almost overwhelmed with such great and copious effu-*
> *sions of God's beneficence . . . and surrounded, witherso-*
> *ever you turn your eyes, by such numerous and amazing*
> *miracles of God's hand, that [you] never lack matter for*
> *praise and thanksgiving.[2]*

In those intimate moments with nature or people, you realize for an instant that you are part of something much larger than yourself or your surroundings. You acknowledge that you are surrounded by God's indescribable generosity. You awaken to the fact that your life is a gift.

> *To be grateful is to recognize the Love of God in every-*
> *thing He has given us—and He has given us everything.*
> *Every breath we draw is a gift of His Love, every moment*
> *of existence is a grace, for it brings with it immense graces*
> *from Him.[3]*

The realization may go deeper during a time of worship when you become aware that God's great gift of Jesus Christ was given not only for everyone, but for *you*. The covenant promises are not just for the child being baptized but also for you. *You* belong. God has made a space for you. Whether you live or die, you belong to the Lord. A joyous surge stirs in you and you want to bow in humble gratitude.

Gratitude is the appropriate response to belonging. Gratitude is certainly central to biblical and Christian thought.

Know that the Lord is God;
We belong to the Lord our maker,
To God who tends us like sheep.
Come to God's gates with thanks;
Come to God's courts with praise;
Praise and bless the Lord's name.

—Psalm 100:3-4, *The Psalms: A New Translation for Prayer and Worship,* translated by Gary Chamberlain, © 1984, The Upper Room. Used by permission.

We give thanks to you, O God . . .
We recount your wonderful deeds.

—Psalm 75:1, *A New Translation*

Let us come into his presence with thanksgiving and sing him psalms of triumph. For the Lord is a great God . . .

—Psalm 95:2, NEB

Let your hearts overflow with thankfulness . . .

—Colossians 2:7, NEB

Be filled with gratitude. . . . Sing thankfully in your hearts to God, with psalms and hymns and spiritual songs. Whatever you are doing, whether you speak or act, do everything in the name of the Lord Jesus, giving thanks to God the Father through him.

—Colossians 3:15-17, NEB

Pray without ceasing. In everything give thanks.

—1 Thessalonians 5:17-18, KJV

People as diverse as Calvin and Merton agree.

God is justly honoured when he is acknowledged to be Author of all blessings; it thence follows that they all be received from his hand, as to be attended with unceasing thanksgiving; and that there is no other proper method of using the benefits which flow to us from his goodness, but by continual acknowledgement of his praise and unceasing expressions of our gratitude.[4]

Thankfulness is "the chief exercise of godliness" in which we ought to engage during the whole of our life.[5]

Gratitude is the heart . . . of the Christian life.[6]

A thankful life is a response to seeing life as a gift from God and realizing that our lives belong to God. God is the Giver; we are thanks-givers.

When I feel the joy of receiving a gift my heart nudges me to join creation's ballet, the airy dance of giving and getting and giving again. Not a value for value received, but a share in the grace of life. Isn't this why we give our gifts, ourselves to God, creation's Giver? Not to pay a debt (who can get even with Him?). But to join His ballet, the dance of grace.[7]

But to recognize the gifts and the Giver we need to be alert and awake; to have our eyes, ears, minds, and hearts open to what is going on around us. We need to savor each moment as though it were a bowl of homemade soup prepared by someone who loves us very much. The psalmist knew that:

Bless the Lord, my inmost self;
O Lord, my God, you are very great.
You are clothed in majestic splendor;
Light covers you like a garment.
You stretched out the sky like a tent,
Extending the roof high over the waters.
Have you not made the clouds your chariot,
Riding the wings of the wind?
You made the winds your messengers;
Your servants, a blazing fire.

—Psalm 104:1-4, *The Psalms: A New Translation for Prayer and Worship,* translated by Gary Chamberlain, © 1984, The Upper Room. Used by permission.

How did he come up with so much for which to thank God? Did he lie on his back in the yard as a kid—smell the smells, hear the sounds, stare at the sky, watch the turnings of the clouds and see figures in them until they became chariots of God? Until the thunder and lightning became God's messengers? Until the whole brilliance of a sun-yellowed sky became the robe of the Divine?

There is a childlike directness to the poet's profundity. His imagination roams the sea; and the sea's creatures, great and small, he sees as God's playthings (104:24-26). Perhaps the poet walked along the river, waded in the streams, sat quietly in the forest and watched animals come to the water, so he could write:

> *You clothed the world with the sea,*
> *Casting water over the hills.*
> *But the waters fled when you rebuked them;*
> *They quickly withdrew at the sound of your thunder.*
> *Mountains rose and valleys sank*
> *To the levels you had assigned them.*
> *And you set limits the seas cannot cross;*
> *They cannot return to cover the world.*
> *Yet don't you also send springs through channels,*
> *Making them run among the hills?*
> *The springs provide water for animals,*
> *And satisfy thirsty beasts.*

> *The birds of the sky alight around them,*
> *Singing among the bushes and shrubs. . . .*
> *I will sing to the Lord as long as I live;*
> *I will sing to my God with all my might. . . .*
> *Bless the Lord, my inmost self;*
> *Praise the Lord! Hallelujah!*

> —Psalm 104:6-12, 33, 35, *The Psalms: A New Translation for Prayer and Worship,* translated by Gary Chamberlain, © 1984, The Upper Room. Used by permission.

The psalmist's eyes and ears were really in love, discovering the world, penetrating beneath the surface and finding God. He realized life as he lived it and was able to celebrate it in thanksgiving and praise. How much more breathtaking our lives could be if we were deeply aware of the gifts of God that surround us and engage us. If we were awake!

Prayer is one way to this recognition. "Persevere in prayer, with mind awake and thankful heart" (Col. 4:2, NEB). In meditation we can wake up to God's presence. In silence we can be aware of our intimacy with God. In solitude we can know our life is connected with Christ and with other people. In prayer we can open our heart, be receptive, make space for God, and begin to give thanks.

FOOTNOTES

1. This story, from an address by the Rev. Eido Tai Shimano, Zen Master, is quoted by Brother David Steindl-Rast in *A Listening Heart: The Art of Contemplative Living,* p. 83. I am indebted to Brother David for some ideas of this chapter.
2. Calvin, *Institutes,* III, xx, 28.
3. Merton, *Thoughts in Solitude,* 42.
4. Calvin, III, xx, 28.
5. Wallace, *Calvin's Doctrine of the Christian Life,* 284.
6. Merton, 105.
7. Smedes, *A Pretty Good Person,* pp. 14, 15.

WINDOWS
TO INSIGHT

Oh! my dear comrades, let us crazy ones have delight in our eyesight inspite of everything— yes, let's!

—Vincent Van Gogh, *The Complete Letters*, B15, III, 511

The Rock at Montmajour

—Vincent Van Gogh

58

GIVING THANKS

It is good to give thanks to the Lord,
for his love endures for ever.
Give thanks to the God of gods;
his love endures for ever.
Give thanks to the Lord of lords;
his love endures for ever. . . .
Give thanks to the God of heaven,
for his love endures for ever.

—Psalm 136:1-3, 26, NEB

We give thanks to you, O God,
We give thanks and call upon your name.
We recount your wonderful deeds.

—Psalm 75:1, *A New Translation*

Come, ring out our joy to the Lord,
hail the rock who saves us.
Let us come before him, giving thanks,
with songs let us hail the Lord.
A mighty God is the Lord,
a great king above all gods. . . .
Come in; let us bow and bend low;
let us kneel before the God who made us
for he is our God and we
the people who belong to his pasture,
the flock that is led by his hand.

—Psalm 95:1-3, 6-7, *A New Translation*

Since Jesus was delivered to you as Christ and Lord, live your lives in union with him. Be rooted in him; be built in him; be consolidated in the faith you were taught; let your hearts overflow with thankfulness.

—Colossians 2:6-7, NEB

Put on the garments that suit God's chosen people, his own, his beloved: compassion, kindness, humility, gentleness, patience. . . . Be filled with gratitude. Let the message of Christ dwell among you in all its richness. . . . Sing thankfully in your hearts to God, with psalms and hymns and spiritual songs. Whatever you are doing, whether you speak or act, do everything in the name of the Lord Jesus, giving thanks to God the Father through him.

—Colossians 3:12, 16-17, NEB

Persevere in prayer, with mind awake and thankful heart.

—Colossians 4:2, NEB

Pray without ceasing. In everything give thanks.

—1 Thessalonians 5:17-18, KJV

Have no anxiety, but in everything make your requests known to God in prayer and petition with thanksgiving. Then the peace of God, which is beyond our utmost understanding, will keep guard over your hearts and your thoughts, in Christ Jesus.

—Philippians 4:6-7, NEB

THANKS IN EVERYTHING FOR EVERYTHING

We must remember the position of Paul, that all petitions, to which thanksgiving is not annexed, are irregular and faulty. For thus he speaks: "In everything by prayer and supplication with thanksgiving, let your requests be made known to God."

—John Calvin, *Institutes of the Christian Religion*, III, xx, 28

In thanksgiving we celebrate [God's] beneficence toward us with due praises, acknowledging all the blessings we have received as the gifts of his liberality. . . . Of the sacrifice of praise and thanksgiving there can be no interruption . . . since God ceases not to accumulate on us his various benefits, according to our respective cases, in order to constrain us, inactive and sluggish as we are, to the exercise of gratitude. Finally, we are almost overwhelmed with such great and copious effusions of his beneficence; we are surrounded, whithersoever we turn our eyes, by such numerous and amazing miracles of his hand, that we never lack matter for praise and thanksgiving. . . .

God is justly honored when he is acknowledged to be the Author of all blessings, it thence follows that they should all be received from his hand, as to be attended with unceasing thanksgiving; and that there is no other proper method of using the benefits which flow to us from his goodness, but by continual acknowledgement of his praise and unceasing expressions of our gratitude.

—John Calvin, *Institutes of the Christian Religion*, III, xx, 28

Thanksgiving is "the chief exercise of godliness" in which we ought to engage during the whole of our life. . . .

Without thanksgiving, nothing can please God. He accepts all service only as it is an expression of grateful thanks for His mercy. Therefore thanksgiving sanctifies the rest of life and the rest of our service to God. . . .

Thanksgiving sanctifies not only the rest of life but also the whole activity of prayer. We can pray aright only if our hearts are pervaded by a true sense of gratitude to God, since prayer must arise from a feeling of love.

—Ronald Wallace, *Calvin's Doctrine of the Christian Life*, pp. 284-285

THANKFUL LIVING

We have been delivered
from our misery
by God's grace alone through Christ
and not because we have earned it:
Why then must we still do good?

To be sure, Christ has redeemed us by his blood.
But we do good because
    Christ by his Spirit is also renewing us to be like himself,
    so that in all our living
    we may show that we are thankful to God
      for all he has done for us,
    and so that he may be praised through us.

—Heidelberg Catechism, Q & A 86

Why do Christians need to pray?

Because prayer is the most important part
    of the thankfulness God requires of us.
And also because God gives his grace and Holy Spirit
only to those who pray continually and groan inwardly,
    asking God for these gifts
    and thanking him for them.

—Heidelberg Catechism Q & A 116

Gratitude . . . is a response to grace. The compassionate life is a grateful life, and actions born out of gratefulness are not compulsive but free, not somber but joyful, not fanatical but liberating. When gratitude is the source of our actions, our giving becomes receiving and those to whom we minister become our ministers.

—*Compassion: A Reflection on the Christian Life*
by McNeil, Morrison, and Nouwen, p. 126

[On realizing that he had survived a very serious illness, Lewis Smedes wrote:]

I was seized with a frenzy of gratitude. Possessed! My arms rose straight up by themselves, a hundred-pound weight could not have held them at my side. My hands open, my fingers spread, waving, twisting, while I blessed the Lord above for the almost unbearable goodness of being alive on this good earth in this good body at this present time.

I was flying outside of myself, high, held in weightless lightness, as if my earthly existence needed no ground to rest in, but was hung in space with only love to keep it aloft.

It was then I learned that gratitude is the best feeling I would ever have, the ultimate joy of living. It was better than sex, better than winning a lottery, better than watching your daughter graduate from college, better and deeper than any other feeling; it is, perhaps, the genesis of all other really good feelings in the human repertoire. I am sure that nothing in life can ever match the feeling of being held in being by the gracious energy percolating from the abyss where beats the loving heart of God.

—Lewis B. Smedes, *A Pretty Good Person*, pp. 7-8

GRATITUDE—THE HEART OF THE CHRISTIAN LIFE

All sin is a punishment for the primal sin of not knowing God. That is to say all sin is punishment for ingratitude. For as St. Paul says (Rom. 1:21), the Gentiles, who "knew" God did not know Him because they were not grateful for the knowledge of Him. They did not know Him because their knowledge did not gladden them with His love. For if we do not love Him we show that we do not know Him. He is love. . . .

Our knowledge of God is perfected by gratitude: we are thankful and rejoice in the experience of the truth that He is love. . . .

There is no neutrality between gratitude and ingratitude. Those who are not grateful soon begin to complain of everything. Those who do not love, hate. In the spiritual life there is no such thing as an indifference to love or hate. That is why tepidity (which seems to be indifferent) is so detestable. It is hate disguised as love.

Tepidity, in which the soul is neither "hot or cold"—neither frankly loves nor frankly hates—is a state in which one rejects God and rejects the will of God while maintaining an exterior pretense of loving Him in order to keep out of trouble and save one's supposed self-respect. It is the condition that is soon arrived at by those who are habitually ungrateful for the graces of God. A man who truly responds to the goodness of God, and acknowledges all that he has received, cannot possibly be a half-hearted Christian. . . .

Gratitude, though, is more than a mental exercise, more than a formula of words. We cannot be satisfied to make a mental note of things which God has done for us and then perfunctorily thank Him for favors received.

To be grateful is to recognize the love of God in everything He has given us—and He has given us everything. Every breath we draw is a gift of His love, every moment of existence is a grace, for it brings with it immense graces from Him. Gratitude therefore takes nothing for granted, is never unresponsive, is constantly awakening to new wonder and to praise of the goodness of God. For the grateful person knows that God is good, not by hearsay but by experience. And that is what makes all the difference. . . .

Gratitude is therefore the heart of the solitary life, as it is the heart of the Christian life. . . .

We live in constant dependence upon this merciful kindness of the Father, and thus our whole life is a life of gratitude—a constant response to His help which comes to us at every moment.

—Thomas Merton, *Thoughts in Solitude*, pp. 40-42, 105, 107

A philosopher asked Saint Anthony: Father, how can you be enthusiastic when the comfort of books has been taken away from you? He replied: My book, O Philosopher, is the nature of created things, and whenever I want to read the word of God, it is usually right in front of me.

—Yushi Nomura, *Desert Wisdom: Sayings from the Desert Fathers*, p. 68

BEING AWAKE

You . . . are not in the dark, that the day [of the Lord] should over-take you like a thief. You are all children of light, children of day. We do not belong to night or darkness, and we must not sleep like the rest, but keep awake and sober.

—1 Thessalonians 5:4-6, NEB

Once I was blind, now I can see.

—John 9:25, NEB

OPEN MY EYES

*Open my eyes, that I may see
    Glimpses of truth Thou hast for me;
Place in my hands the wonderful key
    That shall unclasp and set me free.*

Refrain
*Silently now I wait for Thee,
    Ready, my God, Thy will to see;
Open my eyes, illumine me.
    Spirit divine!*

*Open my ears, that I may hear
    Voices of truth Thou sendest clear;
And while the wave-notes fall on my ear,
    Everything false will disappear.*
Refrain

*Open my mouth, and let me bear
    Gladly the warm truth everywhere;
Open my heart, and let me prepare
    Love with Thy children thus to share.*
Refrain

—Carla H. Scott, 1841-1887

MORNING HAS BROKEN

Morning has broken like the first morning,
Blackbird has spoken like the first bird.
Praise for the singing! Praise for the morning!
Praise for them springing fresh from the Word!

Sweet the rain's new fall sunlit from heaven,
Like the first dewfall on the first grass.
Praise for the sweetness of the wet garden,
Sprung in completeness where His feet pass.

Mine is the sunlight! Mine is the morning
Born of the one light Eden saw play!
Praise with elation, praise every morning,
God's re-creation of the new day!

—Eleanor Farjeon, 1881-1965

I THANK YOU GOD

i thank You God for most this amazing
day; for the leaping greenly spirits of trees
and a blue true dream of sky; and for everything
which is natural which is infinite which is yes

(i who have died am alive again today,
and this is the sun's birthday; this is the birth
day of life and of love and wings; and of the gay
great happening illimitably earth)

how should tasting touching hearing seeing
breathing any—lifted from the no
of all nothing—human merely being
doubt unimaginable You?

(now the ears of my ears awake and
now the eyes of my eyes are opened)

—e. e. cummings, *Complete Poems 1913-1962*, Vol. 2, p. 663

THE CALL OF THE RAIN

. . . Water is always an invitation to immersion [for me], an immersion with a quality of totality, since it would accept all of me, as I am. Some primal urge invites me to return whence I came.

At times I have done so. There is some special delight in simply walking into a stream, stepping into a lake. The child's delight in a puddle is my adult's in the sea. . . .

No rain falls that I do not at once hear in the sound of the falling water an invitation to come to the wedding. It is rare that I do not answer. A walk in an evening rain in any setting is to walk in the midst of God's loving attention to his earth, and, like a baptism, is no simple washing, but a communication of life. When you hurry in out of the rain, I hurry out into it, for it is a sign that all is well, that God loves, that good is to follow. If suffering a doubt, I find myself looking to rain as a good omen. And in rain, I always hear singing, wordless chant rising and falling.

When rain turns to ice and snow I declare a holiday. I could as easily resist as stay at a desk with a parade going by in the street below. I cannot hide the delight that then possesses my heart. Only God could have surprised rain with such a change of dress as ice and snow. . . .

Most people love rain, water. Snow charms all young hearts. Only when you get older and bones begin to feel dampness, when snow becomes a traffic problem and a burden in the driveway, when wet means dirt—then the poetry takes flight and God's love play is not noted.

But I am still a child and have no desire to take on the ways of death. I shall continue to heed water's invitation, the call of the rain. We are in love and lovers are a little mad.

—Matthew Kelty, Flute Solo, *Reflections of a Trappist Hermit*, pp. 117-19

EXERCISES

In Session

In your journal write "I am thankful for _____," filling in the blank with your experiences of today or yesterday. Be sure to write specific things that have happened for which you feel thankful. (Try to stick with today!) If necessary, think back to yesterday, but no further. No generalities from the distant past, please! Take about ten minutes for this.

After completing your list, take five minutes to look it over and say thanks to God.

At Home

1. *Morning Prayers*

    Continue spending five minutes in silence each morning; during that time repeat (to yourself) the phrase, "I belong to God," over and over.

2. *During the Day*

    Take ten to fifteen minutes a day to read and reflect on chapter 3. Read the Reflection on the first day; on other days use Windows, including the sketches. As you meditate on the chapters, you are probably finding how valuable it is to keep track of some of your thoughts and feelings in your journal.

3. *Evening Prayers*

    Each evening write "I am thankful for _____." See In Session exercise for instructions. Then spend a minute or two in silence, looking at what you have written and giving thanks to God.

4. *During the Week*

    I encourage you to be more aware of what is around you. Contemplate—be open to appreciating nature, other people, and your own self. Suggestions:

    Nature: As you go to work or school or are around the house, be aware of all the wonderful things outside. Consider these comments from *Noisy Contemplation* (p. 13):

    > *Children, typically, are fascinated with nature, responding with their persistent "Why?" But adults often stop observing. . . . And so the base of our wonder grows dim. . . . In the beginning, if we are rusty and out of practice, we shall have to remind ourselves to open our eyes, our ears, and our heart to what we see.*

    What you observe can lead to a prayer of wonder. You can include it in your prayer of thanks at night. At times write "I am thankful for _____," and fill in the blank with what you appreciate about nature.

Other People: Try to be more aware of the people you meet and include them in a contemplative glance. Approach people with openness. Include them in your prayers of thanks. Look at people in your family, at work, in class, on the street, and give thanks for them. Consider going to church early and giving thanks for the people you see walking in. And tell people what you're thankful for. They'll love it.

To make this more complete, use the "I am thankful for _____" exercise again. This time fill in the blanks with the names of the people you appreciate.

Next, take just one person from that list and write specific things that you appreciate about him or her. Use the "I am thankful for _____" form. Do this for various persons on your list. Then call or write these persons with an expression of your gratitude.

Yourself: Be aware of yourself as a person God loves, viewing yourself with an honest, loving gaze that reflects the perspective of God. "We need to work self-contemplation into our praying. A morning greeting at the person in your mirror can initiate this prayer as we begin the day" (*Noisy Contemplation,* p. 16). Make contemplating yourself a part of your daily prayer; include thanks for yourself in your evening prayers.

Use the same form of written prayer for yourself: "I am thankful for _____," filling in the blank with what you appreciate or are grateful for about yourself.

In the groups I've led, people seem to find this more difficult than the previous exercises. Somehow it seems like "bragging," "tooting my own horn," being proud rather than humble and self-effacing. Perhaps you have a similar reaction. But remember, this is a prayer of gratitude for the gifts God has given you. Try it! You'll like it.

CHAPTER 4

GESTURES OF GRATITUDE

Christ . . . is more of an artist than the artists; he works in the living spirit and the living flesh; he makes men instead of statues.

—Vincent Van Gogh, *The Complete Letters*, B 9, III, 499

We are surrounded by God's benefits. The best use of these benefits is an unceasing expression of gratitude.

—John Calvin, *Institutes of the Christian Religion*, III, xx, 28

We have been delivered
from our misery
by God's grace alone through Christ
and not because we have earned it:
Why then must we still do good?

To be sure, Christ has redeemed us by his blood.
But we do good because
*   Christ by his Spirit is also renewing us to be like*
*   himself so that in all our living*
*   we may show that we are thankful to God*
*   for all that he has done for us,*
*   and so that he may be praised through us.*

And we do good
*   so that we may be assured of our faith by its fruits,*
*   and so that by our godly living*
*   our neighbors may be won over to Christ.*

—Heidelberg Catechism, Q & A 86

Old Man Praying

—Vincent Van Gogh

71

REFLECTION

I love the Lord because He hears me when I cry and
*   pray. . . .*
Full of mercy is Jehovah, just—yes—but our God spills
*   compassion over! . . .*
So calm down, man; the Lord has given you what was
*   good! . . .*
What shall I give thee, Lord God Jehovah?
*   so many lovely surprises He has given me.*
(I know,) I shall toast the Lord with the cup of victory—
*   Cheers for Jehovah!*
I will do what I vowed God I would do, and I'll do it right
*   among His people. . . .*
Yes, I will really offer thanksgiving to you:
*   Cheers for Jehovah!*
I mean it, I will do what I vowed to God, and I'll
*   do it among the faithful, near the house of*
*   Jehovah, right in the middle of Jerusalem—*
*   (Glory,) Hallelujah!*

—Portions of Psalm 116, translated by Calvin
Seerveld, *Take Hold of God and Pull,* pp. 53-54

Gratitude *recognizes* that a gift has been given, a favor has been done by someone. There is a gift and a giver. But there is more.

Gratitude also calls for a *response* to that gift. We thank the giver with an *expression* of appreciation—a handshake, a hug, a note. A gesture of gratitude completes the exchange, closes the circle, lets the love flow back to the giver.

I remember bringing a gift to a birthday party when I was a child. The birthday child met me at the door, grabbed the gift without a thank-you, ran into the room, and threw it among all the other gifts.

Why do I still remember that incident? Because the giving of that gift is not complete after all these years! I never received the thank-you needed to close the circle and establish a mutual exchange.

Actually, the exchange is more like a spiral than a circle—a spiral in which the giver gets thanked and so becomes the receiver, and the joy of giving and receiving rises higher and higher.

A mother bends down to her child in his crib and hands him a rattle. The baby recognizes the gift and returns the mother's smile. The mother, overjoyed with the childish gesture of gratitude, lifts the child up with a kiss. There is our spiral of joy. Is not a kiss a greater gift than a toy? Is not the joy it expresses greater than the joy that set our spiral in motion?[1]

72

That spiral is evident in many daily exchanges: on your birthday you get something special in the mail, a gift from a friend. You want to sit right down and write a thank-you note. Or someone brings you flowers. Your eyes light up; you reach out and embrace your friend. The embrace is as much a gift as the flowers. The note or the embrace continue the spiral of joy.

The gesture of thanks moves both the giver and receiver to another level. It expresses a unity; it solidifies a relationship. We start out with a giver, a gift, and a receiver, and we arrive at the embrace of thanks. Thanks is expressed and then accepted by the giver. And in the final kiss of gratitude it's impossible to distinguish the giver from the receiver.

When I not only recognize that my wife made this marvelous dinner in front of me, but also say, "Thanks," that tells her:
> *I appreciate what you have done.*
> *I appreciate you.*
> *I love you.*
Our relationship is enhanced, even by that little exchange. The relationship comes from both sides now—she gave, I received; I gave, she received. A gift and a gesture of thanks.

An external expression of thanks—a note, a handshake, a hug, a kiss—*unites* giver and receiver, if only for a moment. We are aware of human solidarity when one person thanks another.

(I wonder whether gratitude can be at least a partial answer to greed and anger. Anger and greed move us to competition, manipulation, grabbing, and clawing. I see gratitude as just the opposite—receiving, encouraging, uniting people. We gripe a lot; perhaps we could say thanks much more and cut through our complaining. Anger separates; gratitude unites. Greed claws to get; gratitude receives. Could we get rid of a lot of greed and anger if we were continually grateful for people in our families, dormitories,
apartments, departments, churches? Making gestures of thanks could create more solidarity in our human relationships.)

Expressing thanks includes acknowledging a dependence on the person who gave the gift. You acknowledge that you are not self-sufficient—that you need the support a phone call brings, the encouragement a compliment gives, the understanding an intimate conversation involves, the warmth a hug provides. A humble give-and-take between real people breaks through a false independence. It acknowledges interdependence: you need each other and the gifts each can provide.

In realizing that God showers us with gifts, we also recognize our dependence on God. We don't like that very much. We'd rather be independent and self-sufficient, make it on our own strength. Dependence sounds so weak and immature.

But admitting we have weaknesses can actually bring us strength. When we admit we are sinners—that we have weak spots, places where we are vulnerable to attack by the evil one—we open the door for God to come with gracious help. It is at the point of our weaknesses that we can experience God's grace, God's saving presence and action.

God is the Giver. We are thanks-givers. As thanks-giving people, we admit that we did not create ourselves. We exist and continue to exist because of God's creative and covenantal love. We belong to God. When we confess: "I belong," we also confess: "I am not my own."[2] We depend on God, the Giver of all good things. And when we receive life and all it contains from God, we can respond with gestures of gratitude.

As gestures of gratitude unite us on a human level, they also unite us with the divine Giver. God offers gracious gifts, covenantal blessings, summarized in "You belong." In response we say, "Thanks! I am grateful!" We embrace God's acceptance of us and in turn are embraced. Or our divine Parent embraces us and we return the embrace as a spontaneous response, an expression of appreciation. We complete the exchange, close the circle, or continue the spiral of joy. Our grateful responses and gestures unite us with the Giver of all good things.

Our social gestures of thanks, like a handshake or letter, correspond to our religious gestures, like sacrifices, worship, obedience. Religious gestures are our way of saying to God, "Thank you for all the good things that come to me from you, the Source of all life."

> *Calvin almost invariably refers to thanksgiving in Biblical terms as a "sacrifice of praise." In the Old Testament ritual, when the people brought sacrifices to the altar, God was seeking, not primarily the sacrifices themselves, but the grateful hearts of which the gifts were meant to be a sign. Under the New Covenant in Christ, since the propitiatory aspect of the sacrificial ritual has been fulfilled and abolished, mere thanksgiving offered as a sacrifice pleases God in a way that nothing else can do.[3]*

This sacrifice of thanksgiving, this expression of appreciation, is certainly present in the Psalms.

> *What shall I give thee, Lord God Jehovah?*
> *   so many lovely surprises He has given me.*
> *(I know,) I shall toast the Lord with the cup*
> *   of victory—*
> *   Cheers for Jehovah!*
> *I will do what I vowed God I would do and I'll do*
> *   it right among His people. . . .*
> *Yes, I will really offer thanksgiving to you:*
> *   Cheers for Jehovah!*
>
> —Psalm 116:12-17, translated by Calvin Seerveld, *Take Hold of God and Pull*, pp. 53-54

Such thanksgiving implies not only a simple word or action, but a whole life of grateful response and joyful obedience.

> *I love the Lord because He hears me when I cry and pray.*
> *Yes—He bent His ear down to me, and I'll talk*
> *   about it the rest of my life!*
>
> —Psalm 116:2, translated by Calvin Seerveld, *Take Hold of God and Pull*, pp. 53-54

> *I will sing to the Lord as long as I live;*
> *   I will sing to my God with all my might.*
>
> —Psalm 104:33, *The Psalms: A New Translation for Prayer and Worship*, translated by Gary Chamberlain, © 1984, The Upper Room. Used by permission.

> *You turned my grief into dancing,*
> *   Stripped me of sorrow and clothed me with joy.*
> *So my heart will sing to you, not weep;*
> *   Lord, my God, I will praise you forever.*
>
> —Psalm 30:11-12, *The Psalms: A New Translation for Prayer and Worship*, translated by Gary Chamberlain, © 1984, The Upper Room. Used by permission.

Offering one's whole life to God in gratitude continues one's relationship with God. Thanksgiving plays a part

> *in the maintaining of the covenant relationship between God and his people. Thanksgiving binds the worshipper to God in the covenant relation because the worshipper thereby recognizes that he has received God's mercy. He confesses having received this mercy and accepts the obligation to live according to the covenant. . . .*
>
> *Thanksgiving can also be used to invoke the saving presence of God, because in recounting the mighty acts of salvation to Israel, the worshipping community pleads the covenant relationship. It was these mighty acts of redemption which set Israel in the covenant relationship*

to God to begin with. . . . God's acts of redemption are the basis of the covenant. They are the foundation of God's demand that we live according to his will and of our prayer that he have mercy on us in time of need. Mercy is well defined as God's covenant faithfulness. Having received mercy in the past had brought about and established the covenant in the first place. Standing in the covenant, Israel could claim the covenant relationship as the basis for her plea for mercy in the future. Israel's prayer rested on the faith that "his mercy endureth forever." Therefore as Israel recounted the holy history, she prayed, "O give thanks unto the Lord, for he is good and his mercy endureth forever" (Psalm 136).[4]

You understand now how psalms can be used in Christian prayer and worship. "Learning and knowing the holy history is essential for those who worship God."[5] So you can understand how psalms of thanksgiving came to be used in Christian worship. In private and public singing and reciting of psalms, we remember the saving acts of God not only in our short past, but all the way back among God's covenant people. And that for us can be an act of renewing the covenant. We claim that history as our history and set ourselves in the continuity of God's people. We also belong to this covenant people. In Christ we have inherited the blessings of Israel and have become heirs to the heritage of God's people. We recognize the pattern of God's faithfulness in the past and find faith that God is still faithful to the chosen people today. And we ask God's saving presence for the future.

We confess our obligation to the covenant. We also remind God of divine obligation! At first that may seem a bit bold to us. But it's just what the psalmists do. They recount and give thanksgiving for specific acts of creation and mercy to remind not only the people but also God of what has happened.

How many things have you made, O Lord!
And you shaped every one in wisdom. . . .
May God's glory go on forever!
Rejoice, O Lord, in what you have made!

—Psalm 104:24, 31, *The Psalms: A New Translation for Prayer and Worship,* translated by Gary Chamberlain, © 1984, The Upper Room. Used by permission.

I will have inner peace again,
For the Lord will act on my behalf. . . .
And I will walk in the presence of God
Among those who live in this world.

—Psalm 116:7, 9, *The Psalms: A New Translation for Prayer and Worship,* translated by Gary Chamberlain, © 1984, The Upper Room. Used by permission.

"Your actions, O God, are the basis for our creational and covenantal relationship. We claim what you have done in the past, and"—and here's the rub—"we anticipate them in the future." That's the boldness of thanksgiving. Recalling God's acts is a way of invoking God's presence. "When Israel remembers before God these acts of mercy then she is reminding God of his obligation in the future."[6]

That may be a little heavy for us, but the psalmists claim the relationship with God, shown in all these holy acts, as the basis for expecting God's creative, covenantal presence in the future. They recount all these acts of God before others, implying that God will do the same for them in the future. God is faithful! As we continue to recite and recount God's acts in the ancient and recent past, we set ourselves a continuity with these expectant people. We renew our obligation—and God's! And we do so openly, in public, "before God's people." Thanks-giving people not only have an inner surge of thanks, or private moments of response, but also give public gestures of thanks.

Worship with people in the church is one way we give public thanksgiving. The church is a place where we realize and celebrate that we belong to God, that God has acted redemptively for us. The church is the body of Christ, the place where the covenant is actualized, the covenant community. The church is also a place where gratitude can be encouraged and where gestures of thanks can be learned, nourished, and expressed.

We gather around the Word of God to commemorate God's mighty works and words. In the sacraments we remember and celebrate our belonging to God, our union with Christ. Baptism initiates us into God's gracious promises and actions for us even before we do anything to merit such grace. We are reminded of our dependence on God for temporal life and for eternal life. God acts first, and we accept with open hands. Holy communion is a meal with God where the menu is forgiveness and acceptance. We participate in the body and blood of Christ and become the body of Christ. The bread and wine nourish each of us and keep the body, that community of Christ's new creation, alive.[7] The Lord's Supper is like a family re-union with Christ. It is a *Eucharist* (i.e., "thanksgiving" meal) at which we experience belonging to God and each other in a visible, concrete way and respond with thanksgiving.

We read the Scripture to learn of God's loving acts. We say, "Wow," "Isn't this terrific!" "Yeah, God . . . !" or "Thanks . . ." in song, prayer, and proclamation. We offer prayer as "the most important part of the thankfulness God requires of us."[8] Proclamation connects God's acts in the past with God's continuing acts in our present lives. We are encouraged to obedience and service and specific acts of gratitude in our daily lives—in family, work, society.

> *Because I belong to him,*
> *Christ, by his Holy Spirit,*
> *assures me of eternal life*
> *and makes me whole-heartedly willing and ready*
> *from now on to live for him.*[9]

The drama of worship telescopes and focuses the drama of our spiritual lives. In all these public gestures of thanks we experience, embrace, and express our covenant solidarity.

Gratitude as recognition, receptivity, and response is a basic attitude and action of the Christian life. We not only recognize and are aware of God's gifts to us, but also continually find ways of saying thanks to God in worship, prayer, and "whatever we say or do." Our aim is to live our whole life as a sacred gesture of thanksgiving, a deep bow of gratitude, solidifying our relationship with God.

FOOTNOTES

1. Brother David Steindl-Rast in *A Listening Heart, The Art of Contemplative Living*, p. 87.
2. Heidelberg Catechism, Q & A 1.
3. Wallace, *Calvin's Doctrine of the Christian Life*, 285.
4. Old, "The Psalms as Christian Prayers, A Preface to the Liturgical Use of the Psalter," 51, 47-48 (unpublished manuscript used by permission of the author).
5. Old, 59.
6. Old, 47.
7. See the challenging discussion in Lewis Smedes's *All Things Made New*, "The Body of Christ" (217-251) and particularly "The Bread and the Body" (238-251).
8. Heidelberg Catechism Q & A 116.
9. Heidelberg Catechism A 1.

WINDOWS
TO INSIGHT

Rembrandt was undoubtedly convinced that by representing the Emmaus story he was able to express better and more clearly the true meaning of the presence of Christ and of communion with him. . . .

We feel quite clearly that in the . . . representations of the Emmaus story the theme is the eternal presence of Christ and the community of believers with him, a theme which is also at the heart of the Last Supper. Hence the reverence and awe of the disciples . . . overcome by the fact that the Lord is really alive, really present, and that they may share in his life.

—W. A. Visser 't Hooft, *Rembrandt and the Gospel*, pp. 26-27

Our Lord and the Disciples at Emmaus

—Rembrandt

THE TEN LEPERS

The story of the ten lepers points to the need for expressions of thanks to God. Ten were healed; nine made no gesture of thanks. It was not that Jesus needed "strokes" for doing a miracle, but that the spiral of joy was not completed by the nine. The one leper returned giving thanks and praising God and was affirmed in his person and his faith. His gratitude united him with the Giver of all good gifts.

On the way to Jerusalem Jesus was going through the region between Samaria and Galilee. As he entered a village, ten lepers approached him. Keeping their distance, they called out, saying, "Jesus, Master, have mercy on us!" When he saw them, he said to them, "Go and show yourselves to the priests." And as they went, they were made clean. Then one of them, when he saw that he was healed, turned back, praising God with a loud voice. He prostrated himself at Jesus' feet and thanked him. And he was a Samaritan. Then Jesus asked, "Were not ten made clean? But the other nine, where are they? Was none of them found to return and give praise to God except this foreigner?" Then he said to him, "Get up and go on your way; your faith has made you well."

—Luke 17:11-19, NRSV

78

CHEERS FOR JEHOVAH

I love the Lord because He hears me when I cry and pray.
Yes—He bent His ear down to me, and I'll talk about it the rest of
my life!
    I was caught in a dead end.
    The cramp of the grave had a hold on me;
    Pain and trouble kept hurting.
    So I called out loud on the name of the Lord:
        Lord God, please! get me out—save my life!
           Full of mercy is Jehovah, just—yes—but our God
             spills compassion over!
        Jehovah takes loving care of those open to temptation
           —when I was cut down to size, He took care of me—
        So calm down, man; the Lord has given you what
           was good!

That's so.
    You got me out of the dead end.
    You have stopped my eyes from filling with tears!
    You have kept me from walking into ruin—
Yes!
    I may walk around in front of God's nose on the earth
        where people are alive!
    Even when I said, "How utterly miserable I am,"
        I kept faith, (Lord).
    Worked up and distraught, when I said, "You can't trust
        a man—they lie," (I did still hold on believing you,
           Lord).

What shall I give the Lord God Jehovah? so many lovely surprises
        He has given me.
(I know,) I shall toast the Lord with the cup of victory—
        Cheers for Jehovah!
  I will do what I vowed God I would too, and I'll do it right
      among His people.

        The death of one of His simple believers costs God a lot;
        And I am one of your serving believers, isn't that so,
           Lord?
        I am your serving believers, just a servant—

        is that why you got me out of what hurt?
Yes, I will really offer thanksgiving to you:
        Cheers for Jehovah!
I mean it, I will do what I vowed to God, and I'll do it among the
    faithful, near the house of Jehovah, right in the middle of
    Jerusalem—
        (Glory,) Hallelujah!

—Psalm 116, translated by Calvin Seerveld,
Take Hold of God and Pull, pp. 53-54

MEDITATION ON PSALM 116

Whoever this fellow was dunned down by trouble—Hezekiah upon his deadly sickness? David when a family and friends' intrigue almost finished him off? or just some simple believer, lonely, hurt, at a dead end—whoever this fellow was driven by God to speak out, he certainly had something to shout about: he had been saved from death, from great grief, from the ruin of temptation! Now he's out there with his wine glass raised high toasting Jehovah.

Some men do not get fifteen extra Hezekiah years or have their enemies cleaned out during their David lifetime, but this believer did, and for the rest of my life, he says, I will live in that reality—God hears me when I cry!

Some people find it hard to cry. When people cry they have stopped defending themselves, pretending to be master of the situation. When pain forces a man involuntarily to moan or fear stuns a person into a noiseless sob, or when simply being stymied too long slowly wettens one's eyes, the person has somehow been broken, his weakness shows, he is humbled.

Sorrow can be denatured, of course, into self-pity, but when this fellow of the psalm was crying, in utterly frustrated misery, suspicious of his closest associates, in pain, harassment, at wit's end, he had the presence of faith while crying to make vows. In fact, his crying became vowing: Get me out of this, Lord! and I'll—

What believer makes genuine vows anymore?

You have got to have an almost Old Testament seriousness and lusty play to your life to make a biblical vow. The superficial Christian life, one lived comfortably, does not know what a vow means. And pietists, who are serious enough, all right, to ruin created joys of life in a legalist concern to meet God's singular demand, would misunderstand a vow as an exercise in righteousness. To many of us, I suppose, a vow looks like a bargain made under duress.

But Jacob's vow, after he had seen the ladder angels use to visit earth from heaven (Gen. 28:20-21), and Jephthan's vow to celebrate Jehovah's victory over Israel's enemies (Judg. 11:30-31), and Hannah's vow for conceiving a baby boy (1 Sam. 1:11) are acts of faith, hope and love, in trouble, glorying, anticipating, praising God for His certain relief! A biblically conceived vow is not a ritual to win favors but is the most rich, imaginatively believing way of offering one's fear, dismay, shame, weakness, humiliation, tiredness, that too to God.

The vowing of Psalm 116 admits without a cavil that evil as well as good comes from God's hand, that nobody knows our trouble like the Lord, and now—you get me out of it for your sake, God!

Let me live! I can't praise you in the grave!
Give me health! I can't think straight and sing so well
    for you in pain!
Save me from my temptations, the stumbling blocks and
    distractions that undo the work of your servant, that's
    me, Lord, your servant. . . .

This is the brusque language of faith we proper believers need to learn at heart along with our New Testament certainty. Psalm 116 reveals that when a believing man or woman is reduced to crying (Psalm 56 says explicitly Jehovah keeps all my tears in a special bottle—what on earth for!), then the believer's life can take on the dimension of vowed passion which is a necessary prelude to toasting Jehovah's overflowing goodness. Unless you live within a vow to God, constrained by love of Jesus Christ, do not expect the jubilant release of cheerleading. No vow, no future. Only a looking backward, a comparison of evils, a trapped feeling.

I love the Lord because He hears me when I cry.

It is not so strange to love someone who really hears, listens to you, because that happens quite seldom, really. Each of us is so respectably selfish in not giving yourself to the other as you give yourself to yourself. Self-gratification weasels into the most intimate association. That is why I love the Lord so deeply, says Psalm 116: my Father in heaven truly listens, heard me when I cried—look at the surprises!

I'm alive enough . . . to have problems, till I die.
I am among men enough . . . to know keen disappointments.
I have enough sense of vocation . . . to be overworked.
I have enough communion of saints . . . to be hurt.
                                        —Cheers for Jehovah!

This insight comes with biblical humor. Lent is the perfect time to consecrate our grumbling, to see the hallelujah in our troubles, pseudo and legitimate.

If you celebrate communion soon, as you raise your cup of blessing to drink, when nobody's looking, raise the cup of victory! a little higher and with a knowing smile say under your breath, "Cheers for Jehovah!" because the Lord's Supper is not a memorial to Christ's death so much as the festive reality of His resurrection though we must wait with tears for forty days or, if by reason of strength, forty years for His compassionate coming.

—Calvin Seerveld, *Take Hold of God and Pull,* pp. 54-55

CONTINUAL THANKS

Prayer has two parts:
Petition and thanksgiving.
Petitioning, we lay before God
The desire of our hearts,
Thus seeking from His goodness
What serves His glory,
And then what is useful to us.
In giving thanks, we own
His benefits to us,
With praise confess them,
To His goodness alone
Attribute all our blessings . . .
Well-nigh overwhelmed
Are we by the outpouring
Of God's blessings,
By the many, mighty miracles
Discerned where'er we look.
How then can we fail to turn
In praise and thankfulness
To God? . . .
Author of all blessings
God truly is;
Receive them we must
All from His hand
With continual thanksgiving.
Make proper use we cannot
Of His benefits streaming down to us
Unless we continually praise Him
And give Him thanks.

—John Calvin, *The Piety of John Calvin* by Ford Lewis Battles, p. 97

TAKE MY LIFE AND LET IT BE

Take my life and let it be
Consecrated, Lord, to Thee.
Take my moments and my days;
Let them flow in endless praise.

Take my hands and let them move
At the impulse of Thy love.
Take my feet, and let them be
Swift and beautiful for Thee.

Take my voice and let me sing
Always, only, for my King.
Take my lips, and let them be
Filled with messages from Thee.

Take my silver and my gold;
Not a mite would I withhold.
Take my intellect, and use
Every power as Thou shalt choose.

Take my will and make it Thine;
It shall be no longer mine.
Take my heart, it is Thine own;
It shall be Thy royal throne.

Take my love; my Lord, I pour
At Thy feet its treasure store.
Take myself, and I will be
Ever, only, all for Thee.

—Frances R. Havergal, 1836-1879

As he was dying, Abba Benjamin taught his sons this:
Do this, and you'll be saved: Rejoice always, pray
constantly, and in all circumstances give thanks.

—Yushi Nomura, *Desert Wisdom: Sayings from the Desert Fathers*, p. 87

LORD OF ALL HOPEFULNESS

Lord of all hopefulness, Lord of all joy,
Whose trust, ever childlike no cares could destroy,
Be there at our waking, and give us, we pray,
Your bliss in our hearts, Lord, at the break of the day.

Lord of all eagerness, Lord of all faith,
Whose strong hands were skilled at the plane and the lathe,
Be there at our labors, and give us, we pray,
Your strength in our hearts, Lord, at the noon of the day.

Lord of all kindliness, Lord of all grace,
Your hands swift to welcome, your arms to embrace,
Be there at our homing, and give us, we pray,
Your love in our hearts, Lord, at the eve of the day.

Lord of all gentleness, Lord of all calm,
Whose voice is contentment, whose presence is balm,
Be there at our sleeping, and give us, we pray,
Your peace in our hearts, Lord, at the end of the day.

—Jan Struther, 1901-1953

WHEN I SURVEY THE WONDROUS CROSS

When I survey the wondrous cross
On which the Prince of Glory died,
My richest gain I count but loss,
And pour contempt on all my pride.

Forbid it, Lord, that I should boast,
Save in the death of Christ, my God!
All the vain things that charm me most,
I sacrifice them through His blood.

See from His head, His hands, His feet,
Sorrow and love flow mingled down;
Did e'er such love and sorrow meet,
Or thorns compose so rich a crown?

Were the whole realm of nature mine,
That were a present far too small;
Love so amazing, so divine,
Demands my soul, my life, my all.

—Isaac Watts, 1674-1748

Three Crosses

—Rembrandt

EXERCISES

In Session

Read Luke 17:11-19, the story of the ten lepers (see Windows, p. 78). Then do the three-part exercise below. As before, the idea is to experience the text, not exegete it. Jot down your thoughts for the discussion that follows the exercise:

1. Imagine yourself as one of the nine lepers who *did not* return to thank Jesus. Why didn't you thank Jesus? (five minutes).
2. Imagine yourself as the one leper who *did* return to give thanks. Why did you return? What was it like? (five minutes).
3. List specific ways you can "return thanks" to Jesus—"gestures of gratitude" you can make in your life (five minutes).

Use your notes to share your responses with others in the class.

At Home

1. *Morning Prayer*

Invocation: "O Lord, open my lips,
and my mouth shall proclaim your praise"
(Psalm 51:15).

Psalm: Read one of the following Psalms, preferably out loud: 3, 5, 19, 90, 106, 145, 147, 148, 149.

Prayer: Silence for reflection on the Psalm.
Silence for "I belong to God" (five minutes).
Close by saying the Lord's Prayer.

2. *During the Day*

Take ten minutes a day to read and reflect on chapter 4, "Gestures of Gratitude." Read the Reflection on the first day; on the other days use the readings and sketches in Windows.

3. *Evening Prayer*

Invocation: "O God, come to my assistance,
O Lord, make haste to help me"
(Ps. 70:1).

Psalm: Read one of the following Psalms, preferably out loud: 4, 75, 91, 100, 104, 116, 134, 136.

Prayer: Silence for reflection on the Psalm.
Silence to write "I am thankful for"
(five minutes).
Give thanks to God for the things you've listed.

Doxology: Praise God, from whom all blessings flow;
Praise Him, all creatures here below;
Praise Him above, you heavenly host;
Praise Father, Son, and Holy Ghost. Amen.
or

Praise the Creator, the Christ, the Comforter,
    both now and forever,
The God who is, who was, and who is to
    come at the end of the ages. Alleluia.
4. Repeat the exercises with the story of the ten lepers sometime during the week. (See In Session exercises for
   instructions.)

A Note:

In this chapter and the next you will be introduced to
daily morning and evening prayers—a form of prayer that
was used in some early Reformation churches. Of course,
this practice of daily prayers goes back further than the
Reformation. It goes back to "the worship of the Temple,
where there was a morning sacrifice and an evening sacrifice
each day" (Old, *Praying with the Bible*, p. 79). It was only natural that early Christians, brought up in the tradition of Jewish piety, would maintain this daily exercise of prayer (Luke
2:37; Acts 10:2).

Throughout the history of the church, morning and
evening prayers have been encouraged—developing in
some monasteries to a series of seven prayer services for
each day, with elaborate music and liturgy. "At the time of
the Reformation the daily offices were greatly simplified,
but, nevertheless, morning and evening prayer remained an
essential feature of the religious life of Strasbourg, Basel,
Geneva, and other centers of the Reformation" (Old, *Praying
with the Bible*, p. 80).

I was intrigued to find in the Reformed-Presbyterian tradition a form of prayer similar to what one finds in Catholic,
Anglican, and Lutheran traditions. By using the structure of
daily morning and evening prayers, a structure which is ecumenical yet rooted in the Reformed tradition, we can have a
sense of history as we pray and get some insight into how
the spirit of prayer can be restored for us today. These daily
prayers may seem rather formal at first, but provide a form
that is simple yet flexible, a form that contains well-tested
suggestions on how to use the time we set aside for God.

Dr. Hughes Oliphant Old gives a rather complete descrip-
tion of the service in a scholarly article,* and shows how it
can be adapted for church, family, and individual usage in
his book *Praying with the Bible* (hereafter referred to as PB).
I summarize what he says:

INVOCATION

The time of prayer begins by calling on the name of the
Lord. In the morning, we realize it is God who opens our
mouths and who deserves our praise, reverence, and awe
(Ps. 51:5). Another biblical invocation could also be used:
"Our help is in the name of the Lord who made heaven and
earth." For the evening, the Protestant Reformers maintained the centuries-old tradition of using Psalm 70:1 as the
invocation (PB, p. 90).

PSALMODY

"At the heart of the reform of the daily prayer services
was the restoration of popular psalmody. The Reformers
understood psalm prayer as an essential part of the prayer of
the Church. They had a high understanding of the psalms as
the prayers of the Holy Spirit. . . . The use of psalmody in
time became characteristic of Reformed worship" (DP,*
p. 126). Two or three psalms were used at each service.

The psalmody of morning prayer puts the emphasis on
praise. "Perhaps it results from the natural feelings of awe
and wonder that come to us all when day begins and the sun
rises and sheds its glorious light across the sky" (PB, p. 85).

"The psalms most appropriate for the evening are first of
all the psalms of lamentation [expressing our sorrows,
angers, and frustrations of the day] and, second, the psalms

---

*"Daily Prayer in the Reformed Church of Strasbourg, 1525-1530" in *Wor-
ship* Magazine, March 1978 (hereafter referred to as DP).

of thanksgiving. . . . Lamentation and thanksgiving are twin themes in the life of prayer" (PB, p. 91).

The psalms end with a trinitarian doxology or *Gloria Patri*. This is very ancient usage. The purpose of a trinitarian doxology is to put the Old Testament psalms in a New Testament light (PB, p. 86). "The Reformers did not blush at Christianizing the psalms" (DP, p. 127).

SCRIPTURE READING

The Reformers understood that they were restoring an ancient practice of the church when they included continuous readings (*lectio continua*) from the New Testament at morning prayer and from the Old Testament at evening prayer. In accordance with this practice, a whole book should be read through from beginning to end, picking up each day where the lesson of the day before left off (PB, p. 86).

"The relationship between prayer and Scripture is very close. It is in Scripture that we find the promises of God that form the basis of our prayer. It is in the Scriptures we catch a vision of the purposes of God and in prayer that we move toward those purposes. Sometimes people have found it helpful to say that in the Scriptures God speaks to us and in prayer we speak to God" (PB, p. 87).

CANTICLES

The Song of Zechariah (the *Benedictus*, Luke 1:68-79) is used after the Scripture reading in the morning, and the Song of Mary (the *Magnificat*, Luke 1:46-55) in the evening. Both songs rejoice in the fulfillment of God's promises, recognizing God as the One who answers prayer.

Two other songs from the New Testament are often used in worship: the *Gloria in Excelsis* (Luke 2:14), in which we unite our prayers with the prayer of the angels; and the *Nunc Dimitis*, the Song of Simeon (Luke 2:29-32), which is also a hymn of fulfillment, a hymn Calvin often used at the close of worship.

THE PRAYERS

This part of the service began as a short prayer (a "collect") and was followed by prayers of the people that the words of Scripture they had just heard would have an effect on their lives. "This was followed with a period of time for silent prayer which was probably concluded by the Lord's Prayer said by the whole congregation"(DP, p. 134).

This time of prayer was gradually expanded. It is suggested that we use the morning prayer time for intercession—praying for the church, the world, and for people in need. Evening prayers are concerned with confession, supplication, petition, and thanksgiving.

Concluding with the Lord's Prayer serves as a sort of summary and conclusion to these prayers.

BENEDICTION

If the service of prayer is held in the church, a benediction should end the service. "The Benediction gradually developed into a very important part of Reformed worship. The earliest orders for daily prayer had a very simple blessing at the end of the service, 'Now depart in peace. May the Lord be with you'" (DP, p. 135).

THE GIVING OF ALMS

"Before leaving the church the people were reminded to give alms to the poor as they left. . . . The Reformers of Strasbourg clearly understood that ancient biblical principle that almsgiving is an important auxiliary discipline to prayer. The Reformers evidently believed that prayer and social concern were inseparable" (DP, p. 136, 137).

A HYMN

Singing a hymn is a beautiful way to conclude a time of worship and prayer. The morning hymn expresses praise. "The Christian evening hymn should be a peaceful benediction to the day, in which our rush and work are put into the hands of our Savior . . . [and] we express our quiet confidence that we are in the care of him whose radiance shall never dim" (PB, p. 94).

CHAPTER 5

PRAYER AS ATTITUDE: THE GRATEFUL HEART

*Why did Christ command us
to call God, "Our Father"?*

*At the very beginning of our prayer
Christ wants to kindle in us
what is basic to our prayer—
    the childlike awe and trust. . . .*

—Heidelberg Catechism, Q & A 120

I thank you, Lord, with all my heart.

—Psalm 138:1, *A New Translation*

*Prayer, for me, used to stand as something separate from other
parts of life. But I have come to learn that real prayer is not so
much talking to God as just sharing God's presence. . . . Prayer, I
have learned, is more my response to God than a matter of my own
initiative.*

—Malcolm Boyd, *Are You Running with Me, Jesus?* pp. 3, 6

*In meditation we should not look for a "method" or "system," but
cultivate an "attitude," an "outlook": faith, openness, attention,
reverence, expectation, supplication, trust, joy. All these finally
permeate our being with love in so far as our living faith tells us we
are in the presence of God, that we live in Christ, that in the Spirit
of God we "see" God our Father without "seeing." We know Him
in "unknowing." Faith is the bond that unites us to Him in the
Spirit who gives us light and love.*

—Thomas Merton, *The Climate of Monastic Prayer*, p. 49

The Bible is Christ, for the Old Testament leads up to this culminating point. St. Paul and the evangelists dwell on the other slope of the sacred mountain. . . .

He lived serenely, as a greater artist than all other artists, despising marble and clay as well as color, working in living flesh. That is to say, this matchless artist . . . made neither statues nor pictures nor books; he loudly proclaimed that he made . . . living men, immortals.

—Vincent Van Gogh, *The Complete Letters,* B8, III, 496

Sien's Daughter Seated

—Vincent Van Gogh

91

REFLECTION

God makes space for us in the covenant family. We are embraced as children. We belong.

We respond by making space for God, by being open to God in our lives, by living thankfully. Gratitude is an attitude of receptivity and response. We are there with open hands ready to receive. Gratitude is an expression of appreciation. We are eager to show our gratitude.

Our *heart* is the personal "place" of such receptivity and response.

Heart has to do with *openness*. When we say "have a heart," we mean "be open to me or to someone else," "be kind," "be receptive." When we "take something to heart," we receive it, take it seriously. When someone is stubborn, closed, we say that a person is "hard-hearted" or "cold-hearted." His heart is like stone, not porous enough to receive anything. It is not open to experience another person's ideas, feelings, or attitudes. When we deal with a "warmhearted" person, we know we will be accepted openly and treated kindly; our sorrows and joys will be shared.

Heart has to do with *depth*. If we do something "from our heart," we do it with deepest feelings. Discouraging experiences that affect us deeply "take the heart right out of us" or "make our hearts sink into our shoes," often leaving us "heartbroken." When we are fearful, we "lose heart." When we "give someone our heart," we give ourselves completely.

Heart has to do with the *center*. We say, "Get to the heart, the crux, of the matter." When we are wholehearted in our commitments, we give our whole selves; we respond from our core. The heart is the center of a person, the center from which we relate to others, the place into which we receive and from which we respond.

Heart is also a rich biblical concept. The heart is where God bears witness to God's self, the place where God touches us and draws us. The heart is where we make a decision for or against God. The Bible tells us that we cannot begin our movement toward God until our hearts are opened, cleaned out, "circumcised" (Deut. 10:16; 30:6; Ps. 51:10; Rom. 2:29). Hardness of heart is a sin—the heart needs to be changed from stone to flesh (Ezek. 11:19). We need "contrite" hearts (Ps. 51:17), that is, hearts broken, hearts opened up by repentance so the showers of God's grace can enter and enrich; hearts plowed up so they can receive the love God pours into them (Rom. 5:5).

In the Scriptures the heart is the place of availability. Paul prays that Christ may dwell in our hearts (Eph. 3:17), the heart being a metaphor for our inner being (Eph. 3:16) where the crucial issues of life are settled. The heart includes our hidden depths and highest aspirations. The heart is a person, the whole person, the spiritual center where we are always available to God.[1]

It is in the depths of our hearts that we are aware of our own self as well as of God. And in a similar way in the depths of the divine heart, God is aware of God's own self—and of us! From our depths we are in touch with the depths of God, or God is in touch with us. God has a Spirit who reveals to us the depths of God. Spirit touches spirit. Heart touches heart. We resonate.

Sometimes when I meet a person, we "hit if off" right away. We resonate. There are sympathic vibrations. Something happens that touches us beneath the surface of our lives.

Recently I visited a woman who had cancer. As we sat together during the few weeks she was in the hospital, sometimes talking, sometimes not, we found that something deep touched the depths of each of us.

That's the same way it is in our relationship with God. God's Spirit and our spirit resonate like two musical instruments in tune, like two tuning forks of the same kind that both vibrate when one of them is struck.

> *"Things beyond our seeing, things beyond our hearing, things beyond our imagining, all prepared by God for those who love him," these it is that God has revealed to us through the Spirit.*
>
> *For the Spirit explores everything, even the depths of God's own nature. Among men, who knows what a man is but that man's own spirit within him? In the same way, only the Spirit of God knows what God is. This is the Spirit that we have received from God.*
>
> —1 Corinthians 2:9-12, NEB

Spirituality, as I talk about it in this book, means this being in touch with our own spirit and with the Spirit of God. Dwelling in God and God dwelling in us. Being "in Christ"

and Christ being "in us." What is essential and deepest in us reverberating with what is essential and deepest in God. Spirituality is the dimension of life that gives it focus, awareness, depth, authenticity, and vitality.

Such spirituality has its roots in faith: that "personal openness to the living Christ as he comes to us and unites us to Himself; that response of a person at the center [or heart] of life—where Christ is. . . ."[2] "The risen and living Christ enters our own lives, grasps us at the center of our existence, and is affirmed in our decision of faith."[3] Faith is our warm embrace of Christ (says none other than John Calvin), the Christ who embraces us. Faith is like accepting a marriage proposal,[4] leaping into the arms of our divine Lover.

Like "a skillful lover the Spirit knows exactly how to turn us on."[5] The Spirit turns us on to our best selves. Our whole person is awakened to God. "Once the Spirit of him who raised Jesus Christ from the dead lives within you he will, by that same Spirit, bring to your whole being new strength and vitality" (Rom. 8:11, JB Phillips). We know we belong together—as God's beloved. We share the divine life. Calvin says it is like a sacred marriage by which we are made flesh of Christ's flesh and bone of his bone and therefore one with him.[6]

> *We expect salvation from Christ, not because he appears to us at a great distance, but because having ingrafted us into his body, he makes us partakers of himself. . . . Christ is not without us but dwells within us; and not only adheres to us by an indissoluble connection of fellowship, but by a certain wonderful communion coalesces daily more and more into one body with us, till he becomes altogether one with us.[7]*

Through faith we know concretely that we are fully and deeply loved. We are God-animated people, impregnated with God. Having Christ "in us" increases our capacity for living, bursting the seams of our humanity. We are lured into being holy, or "sanctified," as theologians call it. We cannot be justified without sanctification following; we cannot be in Christ unless Christ is also in us.[8] Faith is a total response to the presence of Christ within us, in our hearts. God makes space for us. In response we make space for God at the very center of our lives. We make room for God in our hearts.

One way to do that is through solitude and prayer. Prayer is the "principle exercise of faith."[9] Prayer is an intense inward openness. Prayer is not just one of the many things people do in life, but rather "the basic receptive attitude out of which all of life can receive new vitality."[10] Prayer focuses our attention on God. It is a way of being. It is being mindful of God as the center of our faith and life. It is the direction of our hearts. Prayer is a fervent expectation of the presence of God, an openness to the risen Christ who is in our midst (Luke 24:36), an awareness of the Spirit who joins with our spirit testifying that we are children of God. Prayer is knowing and enjoying *God* forever (Westminster Catechism).

Prayer, thus, is not self-centered, but God-centered. It is important to remember this rather obvious fact as we explore spirituality and prayer. For it is so easy to become self-centered and for prayer to become so much belly button gazing. We want to "get something out of prayer." We pray to feel good, to get rid of headaches or heartaches, to solve our many problems, to be happy, to get a spiritual "high."

I once took a course on Centering Prayer. One of my fellow students had been in every kind of meditation group—Transcendental Meditation, Yoga, Zen, Silva Mind Control, what have you. Now she was trying once more, hoping that she could cure her anxieties. It made me ask myself if I wasn't there to have one more "good experience" of prayer. It was helpful for me to read these words from Dietrich Bonhoeffer: "'Seek God, not happiness'—this is the fundamental rule of all meditation."[11]

How we feel is not the test of the value of meditation and prayer. The test instead is in these questions: Is our whole person centered on God? Is God the focus of our lives? Does God dwell in us and we in God? Are we "in Christ" and Christ "in us"? Are we aware that we live constantly in the presence of our loving, heavenly Parent?

> *Prayer means yearning for the simple presence of God, for a personal understanding of his word, for knowledge of his will and for capacity to hear and obey him. . . .[12]*

We can ask God, as Solomon asked, for a "heart with skill to listen" (1 Kings 3:9, NEB) so we will listen and obey, so we will hear and respond with total commitment to the way of life created by Jesus' death and resurrection. When we give our hearts to God, we give not a small part of ourselves but our whole selves. When we say that our hearts belong to God, we give some depth to the phrase "I belong to God." We belong in all possible ways, activities, feelings, thoughts, desires. Even the very secrets of our hearts belong to God (Ps. 44:21). And it is in prayer that we can put our heart in the right place—focused on God, fixed on God, mindful of God, centered in God.

> *The goal of prayer [is] . . . that hearts may be aroused and borne to God, whether to praise him or to beseech his help—we may understand from this that the essentials of prayer are set in the mind and heart, or rather that prayer itself is properly an emotion of the heart within, which is poured out and laid bare before God, the searcher of hearts.*
>
> *. . . Jesus promises that God, whose temples our bodies ought to be, will be near to us in the affections of our hearts. For he did not mean to deny that it is fitting to pray in other places [in Matthew 6:6], but he shows that prayer is something secret, which is both principally lodged in the heart, and requires a tranquility far from all our teeming cares. From this, moreover, it is fully evident that unless voice and song, if interposed in prayer,*

spring from deep feeling of heart, neither has any value or profit in the least with God.[13]

By saying this Calvin wants to save us from what was said by Isaiah about Israel of his day:

This people draw near with their mouth and honor me with their lips, while their hearts are far from me.

—Isaiah 29:13-14, RSV

We don't limit our relationship with God to pious, dogmatic words. Nor do we simply intellectualize our way to God. We can know God not only by head, but "by heart." That

is a very hard discipline, especially for those of us who are "heady" people. But if we are serious . . . we must be willing to engage in the tough and often agonizing struggle to break through all our mental defenses and know our God by heart.
. . . Through the discipline of prayer we awaken ourselves to the God in us and let him enter into our heartbeat and our breathing, into our thoughts and emotions, our hearing, seeing, touching, and tasting. [14]

This does not mean leaving the mind behind in prayer. People seem to fear that if they become interested in the contemplative life, their religion will become mindless. But even Thomas Merton says,

Study plays an essential part in the life of prayer. The spiritual life needs strong intellectual foundations. The study of theology is a necessary accompaniment to a life of meditation.[15]

Yet prayer is more. It may also be necessary "to draw down the attention of the mind into the heart . . . [and] with the mind firmly established in the heart, stand before the Lord with awe, reverence, and devotion."[16] That was said by Theophane the Recluse, a nineteenth-century Russian ascetic. It was surprising to me to find that John Calvin said something similar:

The Heavenly Teacher, when he willed to lay down the best rule for prayer, bade us enter into our bedroom and there, with door closed, pray to our Father in secret, that our Father, who is in secret, may hear us (Matthew 6:6). . . . By these words, as I understand them, he taught us to descend into our hearts with our whole thought.[17]

The two writers, three centuries apart, seem to agree that in prayer "the principle thing is to stand *with the mind in the heart* before God."[18] What a challenge that is! The mind sorts out and articulates what the heart hears, sees, imagines, receives, experiences. And the heart gives the mind insight, sensitivity, and depth. Prayer becomes the attention of our whole person directed toward God, awakened to God who dwells in us and in whom we dwell (John 15:3-5).

"Guard your heart more than any treasure, for it is the source of all life" (Prov. 4:23, NEB). Take care to make space there for God so that gradually prayer will pass from being one activity, duty, gesture among many to an attitude of *your whole existence*—centered in God.

FOOTNOTES

1. Smedes, *All Things Made New*, 183.
2. Smedes, 198.
3. Smedes, 197.
4. Kreeft, *Heaven—the Heart's Deepest Longing*, 93.
5. Greeley, *The Great Mysteries*, 31.
6. Calvin, *Institutes*, III, i, 3.
7. Calvin, *Institutes*, III, ii, 24.
8. Smedes, 184.
9. Calvin, *Institutes*, III, xx.
10. Nouwen, *Reaching Out*, 95.
11. Bonhoeffer, *Life Together*, 84.
12. Merton, *The Climate of Monastic Prayer*, p. 92.
13. Calvin, *Institution of the Christian Religion*, 99-100.
14. Nouwen, *Clowning in Rome*, 104-05, 103.
15. Merton, 108.
16. Theophane the Recluse, quoted in Chariton, *The Art of Prayer*, 61, 63.
17. Calvin, *Institution of the Christian Religion*, 100.
18. Theophane, 63.

WINDOWS
TO INSIGHT

Three Trees

—Rembrandt

A NEW HEART

I will take you out of the nations and gather you from every land and bring you to your own soil. I will sprinkle clean water over you, and you shall be cleansed from all that defiles you; I will cleanse you from the taint of all your idols. I will give you a new heart and put a new spirit within you; I will take the heart of stone from your body and give you a heart of flesh. I will put my spirit into you and make you conform to my statues, keep my laws and live by them. You shall live in the land which I gave to your ancestors; you shall become my people, and I will become your God.

—Ezekiel 36:24-28, NEB

My heart is ready, O God,
my heart is ready.

I will sing, I will sing your praise.
Awake my soul,
awake lyre and harp,
I will awake the dawn.
I will thank you Lord among the peoples.

—Psalm 57:7-9, *A New Translation*

God, in your mercy be gracious to me;
*   In your great compassion erase my rebellion.*
Cleanse me from guilt, again and again,
*   And purify me from my sin. . . .*

Truth, not learning, is what you desire,
*   Wisdom, not craft, is what you teach me.*
Make me cleaner than fresh-flowing water;
*   Wash me and I will be whiter than snow.*
Invite me to joyous delight,
*   Let the bones you have broken rejoice.*
Hide your face from my sin,
*   And wipe away all my guilt.*
Create a pure heart for me, O God;
*   Renew within me a steady spirit.*
Do not throw me out of your presence;
*   Nor take your holy spirit from me. . . .*

Save me, O God, from deadly guilt;
*   My tongue will shout out your justice.*
Lord, may you open my lips,
*   And my mouth will declare your praise.*
I would sacrifice if you wanted;
*   You are not pleased by burnt offerings.*
God, my gift is a broken will;
*   You do not scorn a submissive heart.*

—Psalm 51:1-2, 6-11, 14-17, *The Psalms: A New Translation for Prayer and Worship*, translated by Gary Chamberlain, © 1984, The Upper Room. Used by permission.

SEARCH ME

O search me, God, and know my heart.
O test me and know my thoughts.
See that I follow not the wrong path
and lead me in the path of life eternal.

—Psalm 139:23-24, *A New Translation*

The people approach me with their mouths,
and honour me with their lips,
while their hearts are far from me.

—Isaiah 29:13-14, NEB
(Quoted by Jesus in Matthew 15:8-9)

I do not cease to give thanks for you as I remember you in my prayers. I pray that the God of our Lord Jesus Christ, the Father of glory, may give you a spirit of wisdom and revelation as you come to know him, so that, with the eyes of your heart enlightened, you may know what is the hope to which he has called you, what are the riches of his glorious inheritance among the saints. . . .

For this reason I bow my knees before the Father, from whom every family in heaven and on earth takes its name. I pray that, according to the riches of his glory, he may grant that you may be strengthened in your inner being with power through his Spirit, and that Christ may dwell in your hearts through faith, as you are being rooted and grounded in love.

—Ephesians 1:16-18; 3:14-17, NRSV

A THANKFUL HEART

I thank you, Lord, with all my heart,
you have heard the words of my mouth.
Before the angels I will bless you.
I will adore you before your holy temple.

I thank you for your faithfulness and love
which excel all we ever knew of you.
On the day I called, you answered;
you increased the strength of my soul.
Though I walk in the midst of affliction
you give me life and frustrate my foes.

You stretch out your hand and save me,
your hand will do all things for me.
Your love, O Lord, is eternal. . . .

—Psalm 138:1-3, 7-8, *A New Translation*

NOW THANK WE ALL OUR GOD

Now thank we all our God
With heart and hands and voices,
Who wondrous things has done,
In whom His world rejoices;
Who, from our mothers' arms,
Has blessed us on our way
With countless gifts of love,
And still is ours today.

O may this bounteous God
Through all our life be near us,
With ever joyful hearts
And blessed peace to cheer us,
And keep us in His grace,
And guide us when perplexed,
And free us from all ills
In this world and the next.

All praise and thanks to God
The Father now be given,
The Son, and Him who reigns
With them in highest heaven,
The one eternal God,
Whom heaven and earth adore;
For thus it was, is now,
And shall be evermore.

—Martin Rinkart, 1586-1649

GREAT IS THY FAITHFULNESS

Great is Thy faithfulness, O God my Father,
There is no shadow of turning with Thee;
Thou changest not, Thy compassions, they fail not;
As Thou hast been Thou forever wilt be.

Refrain
Great is Thy faithfulness!
Great is Thy faithfulness!
Morning by morning new mercies I see;
All I have needed Thy hand hath provided,
Great is Thy faithfulness, Lord, unto me!

Summer and winter and springtime and harvest,
Sun, moon and stars in their courses above
Join with all nature in manifold witness
To thy great faithfulness, mercy and love.
    Refrain

Pardon for sin and a peace that endureth,
Thine own dear presence to cheer and to guide,
Strength for today and bright hope for tomorrow,
Blessings all mine, with ten thousand beside!
    Refrain

—Thomas C. Chisholm, 1866-1960

Persevere in prayer, with mind awake and thankful heart.

—Colossians 4:2, NEB

THE PRAYER OF THE HEART

In chapter 2, Windows to Insight, you were introduced to the "Jesus Prayer," also called the "Prayer of the Heart": "Lord Jesus Christ, have mercy on me." (See *The Way of the Pilgrim*.) Henri Nouwen comments:

This way of simple prayer, when we are faithful to it and practice it at regular times, slowly leads us to an experience of rest and opens us to God's active presence. Moreover, we can take this prayer with us into a very busy day. When, for instance, we have spent twenty minutes in the early morning sitting in the presence of God with the words "The Lord is my Shepherd" they may slowly build a little nest for themselves in our heart and stay there for the rest of our busy day. Even while we are talking, studying, gardening, or building, the prayer can continue in our heart and keep us aware of God's ever-present guidance. The discipline is not directed toward coming to a deeper insight into what it means that God is called our Shepherd, but toward coming to the inner experience of God's shepherding action in whatever we think, say or do.

—Henri Nouwen, *The Way of the Heart*, pp. 82-83

THE HOUSE OF THE LORD

In Scripture the house, or dwelling, is presented as a means by which to make our fellowship with God assume a definite form. God also has a house; and the idea of dwelling in the house of our God is the richest thought that is given us, to set forth the most intimate and tenderest fellowship with Him.

To dwell in the house of the Lord all the days of our life, means every morning, noon and night to be so clearly conscious of our fellowship with the Living God, that our thoughts go out to Him, that we hear the sound of His voice in our soul, that we are aware of His sacred presence round about us, that we experience His operations upon our heart and conscience, and shun everything we would not dare to do in His immediate presence.

—Abraham Kuyper, *To Be Near unto God*, pp. 40-41

How beautiful is your home,
Lord of the forces of earth and sky.
My inmost self longs and pines
For the temple courts of the Lord.
My mind and body would sing for you,
To you, the living God!

—Psalm 84:1-2, *The Psalms: A New Translation for Prayer and Worship*, translated by Gary Chamberlain, © 1984, The Upper Room. Used by permission.

THE NOISY HEART

A noise is any sound that you do not want or that comes between you and something to which you have chosen to listen. Your wants are at the "heart" of you. The things you do not want to hear make a noisy heart for you. The things you listen to capture your attention. The things you listen to are those to which your deepest desires have committed your attention. Are they really worthwhile? The noises that keep you from listening, paying attention to, or even hearing what your heart desires can be screened out. What, then, will you listen to? Or, can you stand the silence?

"The noisy heart" has at least three meanings here. First, noise is the load of sound—chosen or unchosen—on your eardrums, . . . the volume or intensity of sound.

A second meaning of noise "in the heart" is the annoyance levels of given noises. For example, the context of a given noise is a good index to its nuisance strength. A train, approaching with bells ringing, engines throbbing, and wheels clanking, sounds like music to your ears if you are awaiting the arrival of a beloved member of your family. The same train is an annoyance if it passes your home at three A.M. every Wednesday—often enough to awaken you, not often enough for you to become accustomed enough to the noise. The frame of meaning, value, satisfaction and joy with which you surround a given noise rules it "in" as permissible or "out" as an annoyance.

Noise "in the heart," in the third place, means the friction that other people cause you in your daily life. I would call this between-folks noise. It may be caused by a physically silent event such as a person not speaking to you, giving you the cold shoulder, or simply giving you a disgusted dirty look.

Between-folks noise is the kind that goes straight to the heart, with or without the human ear. It may arise from competitive, status-seeking and status-holding impasses . . . from longstanding differences in patterns and values in human situations. . . . Nurturing silence in a noisy heart calls for digging around at the roots of what is going on between people. . . .

Purity of heart enables you and me to see God. Soren Kierkegaard, a Danish poet-philosopher of the nineteenth century, spoke of purity of heart as "willing one thing," of having a singular purpose in the love of God and neighbor. He insisted that your and my human cleverness be used to cut out all evasions of commitment, to prevent both the external and internal deceptions that contaminate the heart with the noise of competing loyalties, commitments, and devotions. Commitment is a whole-hearted decision, and a person cannot "by the craft and the flattery of tongue lay hold of God while his heart is far away." Or, in another place in the same work, "As the sea, when it lies calm and deeply transparent, yearns for heaven, so may the pure heart when it is calm and deeply transparent yearn for the Good."

—Wayne E. Oates, *Nurturing Silence in a Noisy Heart*, pp. 11-12, 17

Abba Poemen said: Teach your mouth to speak what is in your heart.

—Yushi Nomura, *Desert Wisdom: Sayings from the Desert Fathers*, p. 58

PRAYER AS PAYING ATTENTION

Simone Weil died in 1943 at the age of thirty-three. She was serving with French Resistance forces in England at the time and trying to live on the food ration of a French workman in occupied France. Through her posthumous writings, she became a kind of apostle of the spiritual life of France during the first decade after World War II. At the heart of her insights is her definition of prayer as attention. *Her French forbear, Pascal, would have approved of this for he felt that the greatest enemy, not only of prayer but also of the whole spiritual life of man, was inattention, drowsiness, complacency, what he called "the Gethsemane sleep" referring to what the Apostles did when Jesus asked them to watch with him.*

"Blessed are the drowsy ones for they shall soon drop off to sleep!" wrote Nietzsche, and his satirical warning holds for those who do not pray. For prayer is awakeness, attention, intense inward openness. In a certain way sin could be described, and described with a good deal of penetration, by noting that it is anything that destroys this attention. Pride, self-will, self-absorption, doublemindedness, dishonesty, sexual excess, overeating, overdrinking, overactivity of any sort, all destroy attention and all cut the nerve of effective prayer. Just as sleep is upset by any serious mental disturbance, so attention is dispersed when unfaced sin gets the ascendancy. If prayer is attention, then it is naturally attention to the highest thing that I know, to my "ultimate concern," and this human prayer means a moving out of a life of inattention, out of the dispersion, out of "the Gethsemane sleep" into the life of openness and attention to the highest that I know. God can only disclose the Divine whispers to those who are attending. Dorothy Hutchinson once quoted a Senegalese proverb which says that "The opportunity which God sends does not wake up him who is sleeping."

—Douglas V. Steere, *Prayer in the Contemporary World*, p. 4

When you search for me, you will find me; if you seek me with all your heart, I will let you find me, says the LORD.

—Jeremiah 29:13-14, NRSV

Cypresses

—Vincent Van Gogh

IN THE COVERT OF THY WINGS

The deepest question that governs our Christian life is that which touches our personal fellowship with God. And in the Book of Psalms, which is the richest outpouring of a devout heart, you see how the inmost longings ever and again go out after this Divine fellowship.

Certainly there is in the Book of Psalms also a mention of the tie that binds us to God as the Creator and Supporter of all things; and of the relation in which by faith he who fears God stands to the Holy One; but both this tie and this relation are still something else than fellowship with the Eternal.

The heart of him who fears God does not rest until it has come to such a conscious fellowship with its God, that between itself and the heart of God there is mutual knowledge, the one of the other— even the clear sense that God has knowledge of us and we of Him.

What we between people call mutual companionship, intimate association, union of soul with soul in faithfulness and in love, is implied from of old in Psalm 25:14: "The secret of the Lord is with them that fear him; and he will show them his covenant."

Even as two intimately connected friends go through life together, and mutually unbosom themselves to each other, and in this intimate walk through life become the confidants of each other's secrets, so it is told of Old Testament heroes of faith that they "walked with God."

And although these are but figures and terms borrowed from those that are used to describe human happenings; and although, when we would describe our appreciation of our fellowship with our God, we should never use these terms and figures except with deep reverence for His Divine Majesty, nevertheless, it is equally certain that God Himself has pointed them out to us for this end.

The Scripture sets the example in this, even to the extent that it borrows pictures from animal-life by which to illustrate this fellowship with God. As Jesus portrayed His tender love for Jerusalem by the figure of a hen that gathers her chickens under her wings, so David not only said that he would abide in the tabernacle of the Lord for ever, but also that he would trust under the covert of God's wings (Ps. 61:4).

And why not?

Is it not God Himself Who in the world of winged creatures has created this exhibition of tender fellowship, as the expression of what moved His own Divine heart? And is not every such expressive, touching picture of love's fellowship in nature a God-given help by which to interpret to ourselves what we perceive and feel, or only dimly sense, in the mystic depths of the heart?. . .

And to express this in terms of passionate tenderness and daring boldness, David exclaims "I will take refuge in the covert of Thy wings." Here soul meets soul; here is the sacred touch; here one perceives, and experiences, and realizes that nothing stands between ourselves and our God; that His arms embrace us, and that we cleave unto Him.

—Abraham Kuyper, *To Be Near unto God,* pp. 38-39, 42

EXERCISES

In Session

1. Silently consider the question "What is prayer to me?" Then write at least four words or phrases that—to you—best describe prayer. Discuss with others in your class.

2. Another question for private meditation and group discussion: To whom do you pray? To "God" in general? Or do you have more specific images of God in mind when you pray? God as Creator? Rock? Refuge? Mother? Father? Friend? Jesus? Comforter? Lord? . . . Think about and discuss your favorite names or images for God. Do you use different images for different situations or needs in your life?

   Discussing this question is meant to have you become more intentional in your use of names or images of God in your prayer and meditation.

At Home

1. *Morning Prayers*

Invocation:	O Lord, open my lips and my mouth shall declare your praise (Ps. 51:15, *A New Translation*).
Psalm:	Read one or more psalms, preferably out loud. End with a doxology—praise to the Father, Son, and Holy Spirit.
New Testament Reading:	Begin reading a book of the New Testament—one that you can finish in a week by reading a portion each day.
Prayer:	Silence for reflection on the Scripture. Silence for "I belong to God" or other phrase that helps you focus on the presence of God. The Lord's Prayer.

2. *During the Day*

   Take ten minutes to read and reflect on chapter 5.

3. *Evening Prayers*

Invocation:	O God, come to my assistance, O Lord, make haste to help me! (Ps. 70:1).
Psalm:	See morning prayer instructions.
Old Testament Reading:	Begin reading a book of the Old Testament—one that you can finish in a week by reading a portion each day.
Prayer:	Silence for reflection on the Scripture. Silence for writing "I am thankful for _____." Spend a few moments saying thanks to God as you look over the list.
Hymn:	End your time of prayer with a hymn.

CHAPTER 6

PRAYER AS ACT

Why do Christians need to pray?

Because prayer is the most important part
*   of the thankfulness God requires of us.*
And also because God gives his grace and Holy Spirit
only to those who pray continually and groan inwardly,
*   asking God for these gifts*
and thanking him for them.

—Heidelberg Catechism, Q & A 116

When you pray, go into a room by yourself, shut the door, and pray
to your Father who is there in the secret place; and your Father who
sees what is secret will reward you.

—Matthew 6:6, NEB

May the mind of Christ, my Saviour, live in me from day to day
By his love and power controlling all I do and say.

May the Word of God dwell richly in my heart from hour to hour,
So that all may see I triumph only through his power.

May the peace of God, my Father, rule my life in everything,
That I may be calm to comfort sick and sorrowing.

May the love of Jesus fill me, as the waters fill the sea;
Him exalting, self abasing, this is victory.

May I run the race before me, strong and brave to face the foe,
Looking only unto Jesus as I onward go.

—Kate B. Wilkinson, 1859-1928

Two Women Kneeling

—Vincent Van Gogh

REFLECTION

Prayer is an attitude that arises from biblical faith and focuses our attention and our whole life on God. It would be wonderful if we could have this attitude all the time. But we don't. We continually need to be reminded and made aware.

> *Lifting up our hearts, we should ever aspire to God and pray without ceasing. Still, since our weakness is such that it has to be supported by many aids, and our sluggishness such that it needs to be goaded, it is fitting each one of us should set apart certain hours for this exercise. Those hours should not pass without prayer, and during them all the devotion of the heart should be completely engaged in it. These are: when we arise in the morning, before we begin daily work, when we sit down to a meal, when by God's blessing we have eaten, when we are getting ready to retire.[1]*

Calvin reminds us that prayer is not only an attitude but also an act. Prayer is an act in which we open ourselves to God's presence, break up our hard hearts to receive the refreshing shower of God's grace. Prayer is a practice by which we allow ourselves to receive God's gifts, to be embraced by Christ's love, to be filled with the life of the Spirit. Prayer as act is a gesture of gratitude that we make.

Prayer is *taking time* to let God recreate us, play with us, touch us as an artist who is making a sculpture, a painting, or a piece of music with our lives, making us "poets of the Word." We need to stop often for the act of prayer. We've explored how difficult it is to take time for prayer, to find ten or fifteen minutes to focus on the most important relationship of our lives. Strange, but true. So we need to be reminded to set aside time for prayer. "Although we want to make all our time, time for God, we will never succeed if we do not reserve a minute, an hour, a morning, a day, a week, a month, or whatever period of time for God . . . alone."[2]

At times in our marriage, my wife and I have set aside certain times in the week for a "date." We've found that we anticipate that special time, prepare for it, and do not want to miss it for anything. Pats, hugs, quick "I love you's" are OK. But we also need extended time together if our relationship is to have any depth. Such times are also indispensable for our relationship with God.

Many people, from many different religious backgrounds, have recognized the necessity of setting aside time for prayer. In the monasteries I visited there were as many as seven periods a day set aside for prayer—periods that ranged from fifteen minutes of psalms, Scripture readings, and prayers to an hour service of worship and holy communion. Calvin seems to suggest nine times of prayer a day: upon awakening, before and after each of the three meals, before work, and before retiring. Such a schedule gives a person a real sense of rhythm between work and prayer that gives each day depth. That's why I have been encouraging *at least* morning and evening prayer for you. "The advantage of early morning is the way it sets our attentiveness for the day. The advantage of evening is the way it reintegrates and settles us down for the night."[3]

"Most important though is not the number of times or duration, but our deciding on *some* time and duration and sticking to it."[4] So, decide on a time for prayer.

And decide on a *place*. Of course, you can pray anywhere, for God is present everywhere (Ps. 139). But it is also true that some places more quickly remind us of God or put us in a reverent attitude.

I remember walking into the cathedral in Assisi, Italy, and all of a sudden whispering instead of talking as loudly as I had been outside. There was a sense of awe.

Churches provide that kind of space for some people. Others prefer to pray outside—by water, in woods, or on mountains. Unfortunately churches are not open every day (although I think they should be), and we often are not able to get away and spend time in the woods. So for most of us it's important to set aside a special place in our homes or rooms where we go each time for devotional reading and prayer.

Many people who have trouble praying regularly have told me that creating a certain place for prayer has been helpful. One woman I know uses part of her son's room while he's off to college. On a table in one corner of the room she keeps a Bible, a hymnbook, a candle, and a cross. Over the table hangs a painting of a quiet nature scene. This space is now used for no other purpose than for prayer and contemplation. She says that every time she walks by that room she is reminded of prayer. Others have said the same about the place they have set up. One woman uses a small corner in her bedroom; another sits at her kitchen table, looking out over the backyard at the trees, birds, and flowers. A group of men who live together have created a space in their basement. When the gas-meter reader came through and asked, "What's this?" he was surprised to hear, "This is our prayer room." One person I know cleared out a long closet and equipped it with an altar, kneeling bench, candle, Bible, and a few books. Another found her private bathroom to be the quietest place for prayer!

The familiarity of one place constantly used for prayer helps settle us into prayer faster and saves our minds from curious wandering. The surroundings can reinforce the prayerful intention of the time we are spending in that place. Our roommates or family members will also become aware that when we are in that place we are not to be disturbed. Such a place can become precious to a husband and wife. Children will gradually sense that this is a valuable space and join in prayer as a natural part of their environment. We need to make space for God in our hearts, but also in our time and in our surroundings.

How we use this time and what we do in this place—*how we pray*—will be unique to each of us. "We need to listen to our own inner wisdom here. . . . We will probably slip into different times and different ways at different moments, as our lives and situations evolve." So along with our discipline we need to develop some spontaneity.

We will probably *talk with God* during prayer. Talking makes us aware that we belong to God, have a relationship with him. We converse with God as child to parent, as friend to friend, as husband to wife, as wife to husband. We can talk with God about *everything*—every fantasy, every ugly or beautiful feeling, every nasty or pious thought, every dream and disappointment, every frustration and achievement. Conversation with God can include all we think and feel. For all of it also *belongs* to God.

We will talk about our sins and failures and anxieties. *Confession* and *repentance* will be part of our prayers. We will also acknowledge our doubts and struggles. We may even end up wrestling with God. We will speak with God about our needs and the needs of others in *intercession* and *petition*. We will bring God our joys. We will offer *praise* and *thanksgiving*.

What happens when we run out of things to say? Is that the end of our prayers? When you are with a friend and you stop talking, is that the end of the relationship? Of course not. In many cases it's possible to be silent with a friend and thereby move to another dimension of intimacy. The same thing is true of prayer. Prayer is an act, but that doesn't mean it must be noisy. It can be an act of silence—of quietly being with God. In fact, some people believe that when you *stop talking*, you are not at the end, but at the beginning of real prayer—"standing in the presence of God with mind and heart." John Calvin tells us, "The tongue is not even necessary for private prayer: the inner feeling would be enough to arouse itself, so that sometimes the best prayers are silent ones."[6]

Silence is an indispensable part of the spiritual life. We need to be quiet in the presence of God. We need to sense the divine Presence not only in majestic storms, spectacular vistas of nature, powerful words, stirring music, fanfare, and applause, but also in tiny whispering sounds and in gentle, delicate stillness. The prophet Elijah stayed still long enough after the noise had subsided to recognize a quiet sign of God's presence (1 Kings 19:10-13).

Like him, we need to be silent in order to be attuned to the quiet God. We often make a lot of noise, speak a lot of words—even to God and about God. If we would stop shouting or even talking sometime, we might hear a gentle sound of love, or simply realize that we are together with God, embraced by the divine Presence. If we are going to be aware of God, touched by God, hear God's Word, we need to be silent sometimes. We need to develop a place of solitude in our hearts.

At a weekend retreat I prayed that I would be more aware of the Presence of God. I was thinking about Calvin's expression that faith was our "warm embrace of Christ." At first that sounded much too romantic for me, too emotional. Then I remembered the Father embracing the prodigal son (Luke 15:20) and Jesus embracing little children (Mark 10:16).

My mind moved from words to an image. I was sitting on a couch, feet on table, before a fireplace. In it was a roaring fire that didn't go out. Whenever it went low, the Other, sitting beside me, breathed on it, and it burst into flame again.

We sat there with cheese and bread and wine. "Cheers," I said, remembering Psalm 116: "I shall toast the Lord with a cup of victory—Cheers for Jehovah!"[7] The Other talked, infrequently and only in short phrases: "I am." "It is I who answer you and look after you." "Quiet." Mostly I was quiet and felt a warmth. Not touch, but "surrounded by" a whole personality. Not buddy-buddy, but a deep friendship. Awe before a Person.

When I want to remember God's presence, I go back to that image. There was nothing "mystical" about that, just my imagination giving me an image. Or was it?

It reminded me of the time I was cleaning up after a service of holy communion. Everyone had left the church. I picked up the chalice of wine . . . looked at it . . . then sat on the floor by the table. Christ seemed particularly present, so I raised the cup of victory to him, taking Calvin Seerveld's advice:

> *If you celebrate communion soon, as you raise your cup of blessing to drink, when nobody's looking, raise the cup of victory! a little higher and with a knowing smile say under your breath "Cheers for Jehovah!" because the Lord's Supper is not a memorial to Christ's death so much as a festive reality of His resurrection.[8]*

Being quiet in the presence of God is difficult. Silence and solitude

> *ask for much discipline and risk taking because we always seem to have something more urgent to do and "just sitting there" and "doing nothing" often disturbs us more than it helps. But there is no way around this. Being useless and silent in the presence of our God belongs to the core of all prayer. In the beginning we often hear our own unruly inner noises more loudly than God's voice. This is at times very hard to tolerate. But slowly, very slowly, we discover that the silent time makes us quiet and deepens our awareness of ourselves and God. Then, very soon, we start missing these moments when we are deprived of them, and before we are fully aware of it an inner momentum has developed that draws us more and more into silence and closer to that still point where God speaks to us.*[9]

We tend to be afraid of solitude and silence. When we get a chance to quiet down, to shut out noise, we find that the noise from inside ourselves gets louder. Stereo! Our minds keep running and go off in a thousand directions. There seem to be so many distractions. When this happens during the silence of prayer, it is best to recognize these thoughts, accept them, but not to linger on them. Let them go, like a balloon. Nouwen urges us to turn this unceasing thinking into an ongoing conversation with God and thus into unceasing prayer.

I have suggested that you use a short phrase (like "I belong to God") as a focus for your silence, as something to come back to after your mind has gone off into many directions. And as you say "I belong to God," you will realize "so do all these things I've been thinking." "I wonder how the children are?" They belong to God. "Will I pass the exam?" That worry belongs to God. "Will I make it through this time of suffering?" I belong to God even when depressed or in pain. "Wasn't that a terrific party last night?" My joy also belongs to God. In some such way the thoughts that come to mind can become part of prayer rather than a disturbance to prayer.

Gradually we may be able to experience prayer also as simply resting in the loving presence of God for a few intimate moments, like we do with a close friend. The quiet God we will find may also be a quieting God, stilling the storms in our lives (Matt. 8:23-27), comforting us in life and in death. The psalmists knew how to "be still before the Lord, and wait patiently for him" (Ps. 37:7). And they encourage us to do the same.

In fact, the psalmists teach us much about the act of prayer. They give us materials from which to build a rich prayer life. "One of the mysteries of the Hebrew-Christian tradition is that so many pieties, so many ways of worship, can derive from the same book."[10]

> *It is a marvel that the Psalter, the product of a small, much despised, often persecuted, always exclusive people, should have been adopted, not under any pressure, but simply by reason of its sheer merit, by every branch of the Christian Church. Here we have indeed a truly catholic volume, catholic not merely in its utterance of every human need, whether of forgiveness or of support or of assurance, not merely in its expression of every human aspiration, whether towards light or truth or eternal life, but catholic in the sense that it is in use wherever the Gospel is preached and the sacraments are administered. Not a branch of the Church but uses it, and that in nearly every type of service.*[11]

I have prayed the psalms with people from many different traditions. And even though I claim to come from a "psalm-singing church," I have found the psalms as much or more a part of these traditions of worship. My prayers with a Greek Orthodox friend include five psalms each morning. And, in

Catholic monasteries I have visited, monks chant all one hundred and fifty psalms each week.

Bonhoeffer, a Lutheran, referred to Psalms as the prayer-book of the Bible and said, "The more deeply we grow in the psalms, and the more often we pray them as our own, the more simple and rich will our prayer become."[12]

The Presbyterian and Reformed traditions have been greatly influenced by the Psalms—perhaps because they were so important to John Calvin. Calvin writes:

> *Not without reason, it is my custom to call this book [Psalms] An Anatomy of All the Parts of the Soul since there is no emotion anyone will experience whose image is not reflected in this mirror. Indeed, here the Holy Spirit has drawn to life all pains, sorrows, fears, doubts, hopes, cares, anxieties—in short—all the turbulent emotions with which [our] minds are commonly stirred. . . . But here the prophets themselves speaking with God uncover all their inner feelings and call, or rather drag, each of us to examine himself. . . . The heart, purged of hypocrisy . . . is brought into the light of day.*
>
> *. . . True prayer is born first from our own sense of need, then from faith in God's promises. Here [in the book of Psalms] will the readers be best awakened to sense their ills, and, as well, to seek remedies for them. Whatever can stimulate us when we are about to pray to God, this book teaches. Not only are God's promises presented to us there, but often there is shown to us someone, girding himself for prayer, caught between God's invitation and the hindrance of the flesh. Thus are we taught how, if at any time we are plagued with various doubts, to fight against them until the mind, freed, rises to God. And not that only: but amid hesitations, fears, trepidations, we are still to rely on prayer until some solace comes.*[13]

Calvin's opinion of the psalms was reflected in the Genevan church. "Under the guidance of John Calvin, the church in Geneva adopted a collection of psalm texts set to newly prepared tunes."[14] Calvin insisted that music is a gift of God and that "there can be no better songs than the psalms spoken by the Holy Spirit."[15] As a result students in Geneva had to practice singing the psalms from eleven A.M. to twelve noon daily. "To make sure the rapid progress of psalmody, Calvin advocated the teaching of the Psalms to the children, who in turn by their singing would teach them to the adults."[16]

Psalm-singing has many beneficial effects. "It deepens piety and personal fervour; it unites the singers with one another, and unites them with the angels. It not only magnifies God, but witnesses to the accord between God and his regenerated children, and it is our illimitable source of energy."[17]

> *The early Christians used the psalms when they met together each day for prayer (see Acts 4:23-31). The apostle Paul tells Christians to sing psalms when they come together for worship (1 Cor. 14:26; Eph. 5:19; Col. 3:16-17). James, in his short letter on the Christian life, tells us to sing psalms whenever we have reason to be joyful before God (James 5:13). . . . Thus from the very beginning Christians have used the psalms in their prayers.*[18]

And with good reason. If we want to learn how to bring all our thoughts to God, the psalms are an excellent model.

> *One of the greatest values of the psalms is the frankness with which they express our most deeply felt emotions.*[19] *The psalms are a series of shouts: shouts of love and hatred; shouts of suffering or rejoicing; shouts of faith or hope.*[20]

> *More than a book, it is a living being who speaks, who suffers, groans and dies, who rises again and speaks on the threshold of eternity; who seizes one, bears one away, oneself and all the ages of time, from the beginning to the end.*

No one who takes the words of the psalms on his lips and their meaning in his heart, who allows the rhythm of their images to take hold of him and their accents to echo through his being, can possibly remain indifferent to them. They may overwhelm or shock, bring peace or exaltation, but inevitably they draw us beyond ourselves; they force us to that meeting with the God without whom we cannot live and who transforms our whole life.[21]

[The Psalms] can be used as prayers by anyone at any time. It is a good idea to memorize some of the old favorites so that they can be prayed often. A psalm that has been memorized can be recited when one lies awake at night, when driving on a lonely road, or while sitting in a hospital waiting room.[22]

I find that praying the psalms out loud keeps me from using them only as objects of study. Of course, we need to study them to understand their meaning. But praying them requires a different use. Saying them out loud has helped me make them my own prayers. I also have found it helpful to sing the psalm—not only to sing the versifications of the psalms that are found in a hymnbook, but actually to sing the words of the psalms as printed in the Bible. Once you have learned some simple "chants," or psalms tones, you can "sing" the psalms with just your Bible in hand.

You may want to read/sing/pray at least a couple psalms a day. You may also want to try your hand at writing your own psalms as another exercise of prayer. You have already been writing prayers of thanks, using this simple form: "I thank you, God, for _____." You could also write a psalm of petition: "O God, I need you _____." Or prayers of anguish and confession: "Why, O God, _____?" Or psalms of intercession: "Our loving Lord, we pray for _____" and praise: "I praise you, O Creator, _____."

These "psalm-prayers" need not be fancy or even poetic—just honest. They are a way of hammering away at God with something that concerns us, or reaching out to touch our Savior for healing, or dashing down experiences about which we are rejoicing.

As we make time and space for God in our lives by acts of prayer, we can learn to pray from the psalms and can use the psalms in our prayers. So much can be, and has been, written about the psalms. I have quoted only a few samples to remind us of their importance for God's covenant people ever since they were sung in the private and public worship of the Jewish people. I am simply suggesting that we recapture the richness of the psalms in our private and public worship. Praying the psalms connects us with this long history of praise and prayer of God's people. We belong to that people. Like them, we find in the psalms a guide for bringing our thoughts and experiences and feelings to God. These are acts of prayer in its true form, acts of speaking directly and honestly with God, or inspiration to be silent before the majesty and grace of God.

FOOTNOTES

1. Calvin, *Institutes*, III, 32, 115-116.
2. Nouwen, *Reaching Out*, 97.
3. Edwards, *Living Simply Through the Day*, 81.
4. Edwards, 81.
5. Edwards, 77-78.
6. Calvin, III, 12, 101.
7. Seerveld, *Take Hold of God and Pull*, 55.
8. Seerveld, 55.
9. Nouwen, 96-97.
10. Battles, *The Piety of John Calvin*, 10.
11. Lamb, *The Psalms in Christian Worship*, 160.
12. Bonhoeffer, Dietrich, *Life Together*, 50.
13. Calvin quoted in Battles's *The Piety of John Calvin*, 27-28. Battles here gives his translation of the preface to Calvin's Commentary on the Psalms.
14. Psalter Hymnal of the Christian Reformed Church, 1959, iii.
15. Lamb, 140.
16. Battles, 139-40.
17. Lamb, 141.
18. Old, *Praying with the Bible*, 47.
19. Old, 48.
20. Gelineau from the Introduction to *The Psalms*, A New Translation, 5.
21. Gelineau, 8.
22. Old, 48.

WINDOWS
TO INSIGHT

Abraham's Sacrifice

—Rembrandt

WITHOUT CEASING

Pray without ceasing.

—1 Thessalonians 5:17, KJV

"Pray without ceasing," says Paul,
Meaning that all men
Should lift to God their desires
At all times,
In all places,
And in all situations;
Meaning too that all men
Are to expect all things from Him,
Give praise for all things to Him,
For to us God gives
Unfailing reasons to praise and pray.
Such constancy in prayer
Applies to private devotion,
But not to the public prayers
We offer in the church. . . .
"True temples of God," says Paul,
"Are we." Do you wish to pray
In God's temple? Pray in yourself . . .
Because the goal of prayer
Is to arouse and bear our hearts
To God (praising or beseeching),
The essence of prayer is set
In mind and heart; or better said:
Prayer is an emotion of the heart within,
Poured out, laid bare before God,
Searcher of hearts. . . .
Pray you may in other places too,

But prayer is something secret,
Lodged chiefly in the heart,
Requiring tranquillity
Far from all teeming cares. . . .
And so speaking and singing
Must be tied to the heart's affection,
Must serve it. . . .
The glory of God ought to shine
In the various parts of our bodies,
And especially in the tongue,
Created to sing, speak forth,
Tell, proclaim
The praise of God. . . .
Private or public—
Tongue-prayers without the mind
Are not heard by God.
In fact the force and ardor
Of the mind must outstrip
Whatever the tongue in speaking
Can express.
One final word:
In private prayer
No tongue is needed,
For inner feeling will suffice
To rouse us to the best,
The silent prayer,
As Moses and Hannah knew.

—John Calvin, *The Piety of John Calvin* by Ford Lewis Battles, pp. 98-100

THE BLESSING OF MORNING PRAYER

The entire day receives order and discipline when it acquires unity. This unity must be sought and found in morning prayer. It is confirmed in work. The morning prayer determines the day. Squandered time of which we are ashamed, temptations to which we succumb, weaknesses and lack of courage in work, disorganization and lack of discipline in our thoughts and in our conversation with other men, all have their origin most often in the neglect of morning prayer.

Order and distribution of our time become more firm where they originate in prayer. Temptations which accompany the working day will be conquered on the basis of the morning breakthrough to God. Decisions, demanded by work, become easier and simpler where they are made not in the fear of men but only in the sight of God. "Whatever your task, work heartily, as serving the Lord and not men" (Colossians 3:23). Even mechanical work is done in a more patient way if it arises from the recognition of God and his command. The powers to work take hold, therefore, at the place where we have prayed to God. He wants to give us today the power which we need for our work.

—Dietrich Bonhoeffer, *Psalms: The Prayer Book of the Bible*, pp. 64-65

Take special care to guard your tongue
*   before the morning prayer.*
Even greeting your fellowman, we are told,
*   can be harmful at that hour.*
A person who wakes up in the morning is
*   like a new creation.*
Begin your day with unkind words,
*   or even trivial matters—*
*   even though you may later turn to prayer,*
*   you have not been true to your Creation.*
All of your words each day
*   are related to one another.*
All of them are rooted
*   in the first words that you speak.*

—from *Your Word Is Fire: The Hasidic Masters on Contemplative Prayer,* edited and translated by Arthur Green and Barry W. Holtz, p. 29

REAL PRAYER

I cannot recall exactly when the idea, and way, of prayer began to change radically in my own life.

Prayer, for me, used to stand as something separate from other parts of life. But I have come to learn that real prayer is not so much talking to God as just sharing in his presence. More and more, prayer and my style of life as a Christian now seem inseparable. . . .

I can no longer conceive of lying to him in proper Old English or any other style of speech. . . .

Prayer, I have learned, is more my response to God than a matter of my own initiative. I believe Jesus Christ prays in me as well as for me. But my response is sporadic, moody, now despairing, now joyful, corrupted by my selflove and desire to manipulate Christ's love. The community of Christ incarnates prayer in its essential life, and my own prayer is a part of this. But many times when I am caught up in egoism and self-pity, I forget. I find in the Psalms much the same range of mood and expression as I perceive within my own life of prayer. . . .

Each of us is a person, with individual masks, scars, celebrations, moments of rejecting God, and experiences of conversion. Our prayers must spring from the indigenous soil of our own personal confrontation with the Spirit of God in our lives. . . . Prayer must be personal, imbedded in the ground of one's own being as a person meeting God.

—Malcolm Boyd, *Are You Running with Me, Jesus?* pp. 3, 6, 8

A MORNING PRAYER

It's morning, Jesus. It's morning, and here's that light and sound all over again.

I've got to move fast . . . get into the bathroom, wash up, grab a bite to eat, and run some more.

I just don't feel like it, Lord. What I really want to do is get back into bed, pull up the covers, and sleep. All I seem to want today is the big sleep, and here I've got to run all over again.

Where am I running? You know these things I can't understand. It's not that I need to have you tell me. What counts most is just that somebody knows, and it's you. That helps a lot.

So I'll follow along, okay? But lead, Lord. Now I've got to run. Are you running with me, Jesus?

—Malcolm Boyd, *Are You Running with Me, Jesus?* p. 11

AN EVENING PRAYER

I'm exhausted, Jesus, but sleep won't come.

My brain keeps whirring with thoughts, and it won't turn off. I have to get up early in the morning, and I'm desperate for a good night's rest. I can't get cool. I keep telling myself to quiet down and drop off, but it just won't work.

I keep rotating, Jesus, first on my stomach, then on my back, then on my side, and on my other side, and on my stomach again. I can't lie still.

The night is going to slip away, and pretty soon the light will come, and I'll be dead tired, Lord. I'm worried, and I can't let go. So many things on my mind. What's going to happen, Jesus? What's going to happen? No, you're right, I'm not looking for an answer. Help me to stop asking. Turn me off.

Lord, bless my sleep. Let me sleep. Help me to sleep. And then wake me up when the light comes, will you? Please wake me up, and let me be refreshed in your strength.

—Malcolm Boyd, *Are You Running with Me, Jesus?* p. 21

WORD

I, who live by words, am wordless when
I try my words in prayer. All language turns
To silence. Prayer will take my words and then
Reveal their emptiness. The stilled voice learns
To hold its peace, to listen with the heart
To silence that is joy, is adoration.
The self is shattered, all words torn apart
In this strange patterned time of contemplation
That, in time, breaks time, breaks words, breaks me,
And then, in silence, leaves me healed and mended.
I leave, returned to language, for I see
Through words, even when all words are ended.
   I, who live by words, am wordless when
   I turn me to the Word to pray. Amen.

—Madeleine L'Engle, *The Weather of the Heart*, p. 60

Our Lord and the Disciples at Emmaus

—Rembrandt

124

WORD, SILENCE

It seems possible to establish a few guidelines.

In the first place, we have to pay careful attention to the word of God as it is written in the holy scriptures. St. Augustine was converted when he responded to the words of a child saying: "take and read, take and read." When he took the Bible and started reading the page on which he opened it, he felt that the words he read were directly spoken to him.

To take the holy scriptures and read them is the first thing we have to do to open ourselves to God's call. Reading the scriptures is not as easy as it seems since in our academic world we tend to make anything and everything we read subject to analysis and discussion. But the word of God should lead us first of all to contemplation and meditation. Instead of taking the words apart, we should bring them together in our innermost being; instead of wondering if we agree or disagree, we should wonder which words are directly spoken to us and connect directly with our most personal story. Instead of thinking about the words as potential subjects for an interesting dialogue or paper, we should be willing to let them penetrate into the most hidden corners of our heart, even to those places where no other word has yet found entrance. Then and only then can the word bear fruit as seed sown in rich soil. Only then can we really "hear and understand" (Matthew 13:23).

Secondly we simply need quiet time in the presence of God. Although we want to make all our time, time for God, we will never succeed if we do not reserve a minute, an hour, a morning, a day, a week, a month or whatever period of time for God and him alone. This asks for much discipline and risk taking because we always seem to have something more urgent to do and "just sitting there" and "doing nothing" often disturbs us more than it helps. But there is no way around this. Being useless and silent in the presence of our God belongs to the core of all prayer. In the beginning we often hear our own unruly inner noises more loudly than God's voice. This is at times very hard to tolerate. But slowly, very slowly, we discover that the silent time makes us quiet and deepens our awareness of ourselves and God. Then, very soon, we start missing these moments when we are deprived of them, and before we are fully aware of it an inner momentum has developed that draws us more and more into silence and closer to that still point where God speaks to us.

Contemplative reading of the holy scriptures and silent time in the presence of God belong closely together. The word of God draws us into silence; silence makes us attentive to God's word. The word of God penetrates through the thick of human verbosity to the silent center of our heart; silence opens in us the space where the word can be heard. Without reading the word, silence becomes stale, and without silence, the word loses its re-creative power. The word leads to silence and silence to the word. The word is born in silence, and silence is the deepest response to the word.

—Henri Nouwen, *Reaching Out,* pp. 96-97

FINDING POCKETS OF SILENCE IN THE DAY'S WORK

During your day you will be hard pressed to find silence on the job, particularly if you work in a large city, a large industry, a large business. The nearest thing to a place of quietness many people find is in the restroom. A place of work can easily be portrayed as a place where people talk without speaking and hear without listening. . . .

If you are committed to nurturing silence, you will measure your day in terms of that commitment. For example, you may choose some day to eat your lunch alone in your office, behind a stack of boxes in a warehouse, or in a little-used park near your place of work. You may use your coffee break to go for a walk. You stop only by the water fountain to rehydrate yourself. I have discovered that a long brisk walk to lunch on the main street of my city away from our hospital teaching clinic gives me exercise, frees me of seeing many people I have to talk with or listen to, and gives me a time to let my soul catch up with my body.

I can recall how the massive noise of a cotton mill shut out all conversation. We had to learn how to read lips, to make signs and signals of communication with our hands, head, and feet, etc. Yet the massive noise was an overcast for all other noises and I experienced profound times of inner quietness in my own heart. I felt the growth of a mystical consciousness start in my life at that time. On the job I have now, I wondered why on earth the hospital had installed a music inlet into my office. I now know that it was to create an overcast of pleasant sound to maintain a degree of privacy from voices through thin walls. Personally, I prefer to have walls that are sound insulated. More recently this has been done. It was difficult to function with that music going. However, I have told you what my generation is now. The present group of younger persons are accustomed to television and radio going while they are working. They do not live comfortably with the sounds of silence. I certainly am not putting them down for this. They have their own mystique. Possibly the music covers out all other noises and enables them to commune within as the machine noises in the cotton mills did for me when I was young.

—Wayne Oates, *Nurturing Silence in a Noisy Heart*, pp. 48-49

It was said about Abba Agathon that for three years he carried a pebble around in his mouth until he learned to be silent.

—Yushi Nomura, *Desert Wisdom: Sayings from the Desert Fathers*, p. 5

CALVIN ON MEDITATION

As it will become clear in our presentation, the center of devotional meditation is in our prayers and our study of the Scriptures. This is the case with public preaching of the Word and with private study of the Bible. Meditation is not identical either with prayer or the reading and preaching of Scriptures. Meditation cannot be separated from either. Meditation often leads to prayer and should always accompany prayer. Calvin does not seem to have in mind any particular discipline or technique of meditation. We find nothing in Calvin like the spiritual exercises of Ignatius Loyola. The closest thing to this which we find is the devotional reading of the Scripture or perhaps more particularly the devotional use of the psalms in both public and private worship. The study of Scripture and the discipline of prayer obviously merge when the psalms are used in prayer. The meditation on the psalms as a devotional practice is probably as close to any technique which we would find. . . .

Calvin's commentary implies that meditation on the law is synonymous with the study of the Scripture in general. . . . To Calvin the study of the law would have meant listening to the Word of God with all the literary, grammatical, and historical tools that were available to him. It would have included, of course, the Ancient languages of Greek and Hebrew, a knowledge of classical rhetoric and ancient history. Calvin did not mean by meditation some sort of pious contemplation over, beyond and beside the intellectual thinking about Scripture. He meant an intelligent search for the meaning of the text. For Calvin there is no question of using Scriptures as a mantra. Scripture has meaning and it needs to be heard and understood. . . .

For Calvin meditation has a particular content. It is not an emptying of the mind but rather filling it. That with which Calvin is most concerned to fill his mind in meditation is the remembrance of the work of God. Sometimes this means the works of Creation, but most often it means the works of Redemption. It is very closely related to meditation on the glory of God or the faithfulness of God.

We are to devote the [Lord's] day to meditating on the divine works. The whole day is devoted to worship so that we can disengage ourselves from the cares of the world and apply ourselves to the praises of God. It is obviously true that the sort of meditation Calvin has in mind does involve emptying one's mind of distractions. In his chapter on prayer in the Institutes, there is a section on the importance of concentration in prayer. This is quite different however from the sort of concentration taught by the masters of Zen or the transcending of thought practiced by Hindu meditation groups. For Calvin meditation very specifically has content. It is remembering holy history.

Calvin criticizes the spiritualists and anabaptists of his day who despised "outward means." He probably had very specifically in mind such people as Casper Swenckfeld who . . . was opposed to any outward forms of prayer and advocated what he called a purely spiritual worship. Calvin recognized the importance of having aids to meditating on the divine works. Reading through the Scriptures would certainly be one of the aids to our meditation. That is certainly one of the reasons the daily prayer services of Geneva included a regular reading through of the Old and New Testaments. . . . Again we want to say that the use of a psalm as an aid to meditation is quite different from the use of a mantra. The psalm is used to inspire the remembering of holy history.

One sees a real distinction between the kind of philosophical meditation which tries to penetrate to the essence of God and the sort of meditation which observes with the senses and considers with the mind the method of God's works.

—Hughes Oliphant Old, "Meditation in
Calvin's Commentary on the Psalms"

MY GOD, IS ANY HOUR SO SWEET

My God, is any hour so sweet,
  From blush of morn to evening star,
As that which calls me to Thy feet,
  The hour of prayer?

Then is my strength by Thee renewed;
  Then are my sins by Thee forgiven;
Then dost Thou cheer my solitude
  With hopes of heaven.

No words can tell what sweet relief
  There for my every want I find,
What strength for warfare, balm for grief,
  What peace of mind.

Hushed is each doubt, gone every fear;
  My spirit seems in heaven to stay;
And e'en the penitential tear
  Is wiped away.

Lord, till I reach yon blissful shore,
  No privilege so dear shall be
As thus my inmost soul to pour
  In prayer to Thee.

—Charlotte Elliott, 1789-1871

JOINING THE CONVERSATION

Prayer is a conversation with God. This is how most people would define prayer. What they would mean is a conversation that we are expected to begin. . . .

In complete contrast, Israel's God was all initiative. The living God acted and spoke first, choosing, wooing, calling, inviting. . . . The whole of existence . . . is a conversation which God begins. In prayer, as in life, we are the ones who answer. God touches us, God speaks to us, God moves us, God reveals truth to us, and life and prayer is our response.

In prayer, we are never "getting a conversation going" with God. We are continuing a conversation which God has begun. . . . For many, [this] amounts to a radical revisioning of the whole enterprise of prayer. . . . It gives priority to attention and receptivity. . . . [It also] compels us to reckon with God as giver and lover, rather than as taskmaster. It is pathetically common for people to be operating under the tacit assumption that prayer is a duty, a requirement, a task. . . .

What if God does not demand prayer as much as gives prayer? . . . What if praying means opening ourselves to the gift of God's own self and presence? What if our part in prayer is primarily letting God be giver? Suppose prayer is not a duty but the opportunity to experience healing and transforming love? . . . Instead of prayer being another demand that threatens to deplete your energy further, it could become the place of replenishment and access to the love which gives life meaning. . . .

Our prayer is not making conversation with God. It is joining the conversation that is already going on in God.

—Martin L. Smith, *The Word Is Very Near You:*
A Guide to Praying with Scripture, pp. 14, 18-21

*Boats on the Beach
at Saintes-Maries*

—Vincent Van Gogh

131

EXERCISES

In Session

1. Here's a brief summary of the "acts of prayer" we've been practicing (add any ideas that occur to you):
   a. talking with God alone or with a group or in public worship
   b. saying our morning and evening prayers at home
   c. observing silence
      —to begin each group session
      —to contemplate a biblical story or text
      —to focus our attention on God, using a word or phrase
      —to write/offer prayers of thanksgiving
   d. singing
   e. singing/praying/the Psalms
   f. writing psalms of our own
   g. being aware of nature, other people, ourselves
   h. being aware of the presence of God
   i. saying the Lord's Prayer
   j. contemplating art (drawings in each chapter)
   k. reflecting on various readings
   l. listening to music
2. Now that you've explored a few acts of prayer, it's time to develop your own personal prayer discipline—to choose a time, place, and a form of prayer that will help you pray more deeply and make space for God more readily. Develop a plan that you believe you can follow for a week. Be gentle with yourself—don't make your discipline so demanding that you will fail and be disappointed. But do not be lazy either. Make the discipline something you can gradually build on as you grow in spirituality and prayer.

   Take fifteen minutes, now, to write your discipline into your journal. Decide:
      —WHEN? (What time? How long?)
      —WHERE?
      —WHAT? (kinds of prayer, readings, etc.)
      —HOW? (posture)
   End this time with a prayer asking God for the courage and discipline to pray just as you have planned. When you're finished, discuss your discipline with one other person in the group.

At Home

   Practice, each day, the discipline you just wrote out. Be ready to discuss what happened during the week so you can revise your discipline next week, if necessary. Record in your journal your reactions to practicing your discipline. Be sure to bring the journal to the next group meeting.

   Also, please read chapter 6. Consider writing some psalms of your own, using the form suggested in this chapter.

7

CHAPTER 7

WRESTLING WITH GOD

How does the knowledge
of God's creation and providence help us?

We can be patient when things go against us,
   thankful when things go well,
   and for the future we can have
   good confidence in our faithful God and Father
   that nothing will separate us from his love.
   All creatures are so completely in his hand
     that without his will
     they can neither move nor be moved.

                   —Heidelberg Catechism, Q & A 28

In this print I have tried to express . . . what seems to me one of the strongest proofs of the existence . . . of God and eternity—certainly in the infinitely touching expression of such a little old man, which he himself is perhaps unconscious of, when he is sitting quietly in his corner by the fire. At the same time there is something precious, something noble, which cannot be destined for the worms. . . . This is far from theology, simply the fact that the poorest little woodcutter or peasant on the heath or miner can have moments of emotion and inspiration which give him a feeling of an eternal home, and of being close to it.

          —Vincent Van Gogh, *The Complete Letters*, 248, I, 495

My God, my God, why abandon me?
   My groaning words do not help me at all!
All day I call, but you do not answer;
   All night, but I find no rest. . . .
Do not be far from me!
   For trouble is near; there is no one to help.

     —Psalm 22:1-2, 11, *The Psalms: A New Translation for*
Prayer and Worship, translated by Gary Chamberlain,
© 1984, The Upper Room. Used by permission.

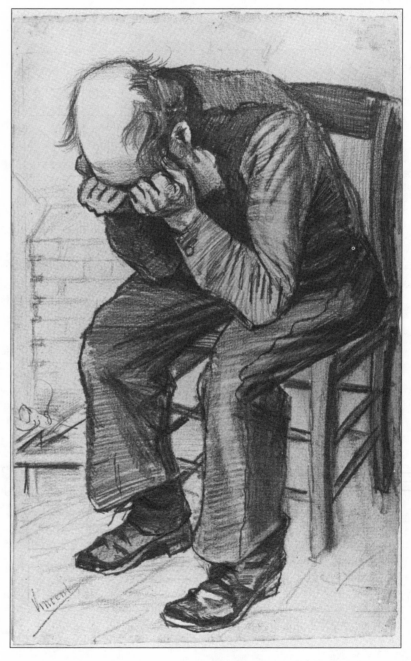

At Eternity's Gate

—Vincent Van Gogh

REFLECTION

A woman who was dying of cancer told me she got angry at times. I asked whether she ever got angry at God. After some hesitation she admitted that she did. "Did you ever tell God?" We spent time talking about that, realizing that some of God's dearest servants got angry with God. After she died, her son told me how helpful it had been for her to express her anger at God and to God.

This woman's struggle is experienced, if not expressed very much, by many people. Maybe you've felt it—even if only for a moment, in the dark of night, when you were alone like Jacob (Gen. 32:24-30). "Our first response to such feelings is to hide them from God in the belief that they have no place in our spiritual life. In so doing, however, we limit our relationship with God to pious moments or sentimental hours. Our spiritual life then loses strength and power and quickly becomes divorced from the issues that really matter."[1] If we believe in God, if we really belong to God, we may find ourselves struggling with God. If we listen attentively to our hearts, to the cries of our friends and our angry world, we may find ourselves in conflict with God. We believe in a God who is mercy and justice, yet we see so much injustice. We believe in a God who is wholeness and salvation, yet we see so much brokenness and suffering. We believe in a God of love, yet we see so much hatred. These conflicts raise questions. And to ask these questions not as academic riddles but

as a life demand is to wrestle with God. To shout "Why?" at the heavens in protest is to wrestle with God.

We all have probably questioned God at some time—even if only for a moment. Whenever I do that—protest against God, shout "Why!" at God, get angry with the divine Majesty, struggle with God about the direction of my life or about the seeming divine unconcern—I think it is a lack of faith, indicating my distance from God. It seems to call for repentance.

But though I think that way, I don't feel that way. When I struggle, it feels like I am close to God, as close as when I argue with my family or friends, as when my two sons used to wrestle together. It feels like God is close—just as God was close to Jacob when he wrestled "with God and men" (Gen. 32:28); or to Job when he complained (Job 2:7-10; 3:1-5, 11-13; 10:8-9); or to Jeremiah when he challenged (Jer. 15:15-16, 18; 20:7-8, 10, 13, 15, 18); or to Hannah when she cried out (1 Sam. 1); or to the psalmist when he protested (Ps. 22). Confronting God is part of the biblical tradition. When we read the Psalms, the prophets, and other Scriptures, we find people wrestling with God.

Were those people who wrestled with God far from God? Or does their struggling show how close to God they were? Is "the refusal to accept the harshness of God's ways in the name of his love . . . an authentic form of prayer," as the Jewish philosopher Abraham Heschel claims?[2] Is it true, as one Christian writer puts it, that "when I can only relate to God in terms of submission, I am much more distant from him than when I can question his decrees"?[3]

Jacob received the name "Israel" because, as his divine opponent said, "you wrestled with God and with men, and prevailed!" And he received a blessing. He emerged from the struggle physically lame but spiritually regenerated: "I saw God face to face and my life is spared" (Gen. 32:30). The name *Israel*, the "God-Wrestler," was later given to a whole race of people—a people whose protests often mixed with their praise, not as a sign of lack of faith, but as a sign of depth of faith, as an expression of love. And Christians do not shun that name; we call ourselves the new Israel, the new God-wrestlers! God is our lover. But we struggle with our divine lover just as we struggle with our human lovers. Because we know there's a basis of trust beneath our differences and disagreements and disappointments, we're able to argue with those we love as well as relate warmly to them.

At the dinner table one night I was being rather harsh and irritable with the family. At last one of my teenage sons said, "Dad, why don't you just shut up!" And then he cried. For some reason I accepted his admonition—maybe because he was right. He could risk those words because we had a more basic relationship. Instead of alienating us, his outburst brought us closer together. It put our communication on a deeper and more mature level.

Speaking our anger is a form of communication. It may even presuppose love between persons. I dare to be myself, to reveal what I really feel to those whom I love.

Could it be the same with God? The closer we are to God, the more we dare to say what's going on in our minds and in our guts? We belong to God—even with our negative, hostile attitudes! Somehow the psalmists, Jacob, Job, Jeremiah, and Hannah dared. Even our Savior struggled with God in the Garden of Gethsemane and sweat blood. When he said,

"Thy will be done," he was not tossing off a glib phrase to justify a lazy acceptance of what was happening. He said those words only in and after a terrible struggle. We almost hesitate to read that poignant story, lest we intrude on the private agony of Jesus. Yet there it is for us to read (Matt. 26:36-46). Jesus in the garden; and on the cross, quoting the psalmist's protest: "My God, my God, why. . . !" Who can watch without seeing all our cries, our whys, our anguished shouts embraced in that terrible moment?

None of these are easy pious words, but deep expressions of anguish. Yet we never feel that these people are cut off from God's love. In a strange way we feel that God is with them—not in spite of their words, but because of them. Their words keep the connection. Their words are (dare we say it?) prayers! If we cannot say these words to our loving Parent, to whom can we say them? Do we love God enough to give God *everything* in our minds and hearts? If we do not express what is there, we risk closing the doors of our openness and awareness to God and withdrawing from our relationship with God.

> *When I need a doctor's care, I show him my wounds. I do not hide them and show him only what is healthy. Refusing to call hatred and resentment by their real names would be hiding my wounds from the Lord.[4]*

Anger might not be the best way of communicating, but it is our way from time to time. These feelings are ours, like it or not, proud of them or not. So we do not have to mince words with God.

Surprisingly, our angry words can be a way of coming back to God rather than distancing ourselves from God. The wrestle may be like a violent embrace. And once we wrestle, we may go back into life, limping but renewed—like Jacob, physically lame but spiritually regenerated. Making war was like making love.[5] And conflict with God was turned into praise.

The last glimpse we get of Israel is of a man limping home, blessed, against the brightness of the dawn.[6] He knew he had met God; and that knowledge stayed with him the rest of his life, as he limped along. He had struggled with himself, with his lies and his own questions, with his relationship with Esau ("with men");[7] and he had wrestled with God—and prevailed! He had seen God face to face and lived.

What was a personal struggle for Jacob became a cosmic struggle in Jesus. God and humanity are in open conflict in Jesus. It is awful. He suffers so with his people that he can hardly take it. And he seems to also struggle with God. The conflict of the ages comes together in that wrestling in the garden and in the anguished "Why?" from the cross. Jesus' anguished "Why?" as he suffers and struggles with God is somehow also a cry of faith. And at the end of the struggle, the cry of faith becomes a cry of affirmation: "Into your hands, O God, I commend my spirit." He has borne the struggle of God and of people—and prevailed.

We know he prevailed, for we get yet another glimpse of Jesus—staggering on broken feet out of the tomb toward the dawn of the resurrection.[8] The conflict of the cross becomes the companionship and comfort of the resurrection. In Christ we can face God and live; we can encounter God and be blessed. We dare give ourselves into the violent embrace of God—if only for a moment. We can be so close to God in Christ that we can cling and challenge, surrender and protest, worship and wrestle.

As we learn more about spirituality and prayer, about what it really means to belong to God, we may dare to wrestle with God—and end up with a covenantal hug!

FOOTNOTES
1. Nouwen in the Introduction to Wolff's *May I Hate God?*, 2.
2. Nouwen, *The Genesee Diary*, 121-122.
3. Nouwen, 122.
4. Wolff, 43.
5. Waskow, *Godwrestling*, 6-7.
6. Beuchner, *The Magnificent Defeat*, 18.
7. Waskow, 6-7.
8. Beuchner, 18.

WINDOWS
TO INSIGHT

"The Roots" shows some tree roots on sandy ground. . . . I tried to put sentiment into the land-scape . . . the convulsive, passion-ate clinging to the earth, and yet being half torn up by the storm. I wanted to express something of the struggle for life . . . in the black, gnarled and knotty roots.

—Vincent Van Gogh,
The Complete Letters, 195, I, 360

The Roots

—Vincent Van Gogh

JACOB WRESTLING WITH GOD

The same night he got up and took his two wives, his two maids, and his eleven children, and crossed the ford of the Jabbok. He took them and sent them across the stream, and likewise everything that he had. Jacob was left alone; and a man wrestled with him until daybreak. When the man saw that he did not prevail against Jacob, he struck him on the hip socket; and Jacob's hip was put out of joint as he wrestled with him. Then he said, "Let me go, for the day is breaking." But Jacob said, "I will not let you go, unless you bless me." So he said to him, "What is your name?" And he said, "Jacob." Then the man said, "You shall no longer be called Jacob but Israel, for you have striven with God and with humans, and have prevailed." Then Jacob asked him, "Please tell me your name." But he said, "Why is it that you ask my name?" And there he blessed him. So Jacob called the place Peniel, saying, "For I have seen God face to face, and yet my life is preserved." The sun rose upon him as he passed Peniel, limping because of his hip. Therefore to this day the Israelites do not eat the thigh muscle that is on the hip socket, because he struck Jacob on the hip socket at the thigh muscle.

—Genesis 32:22-32, NRSV

GODWRESTLING

I wrestled again with my brother last week,
First time since I was twelve and Grandma stopped us:
"She won't even let us fight!" we yelled, embracing,
But she said talking was nicer.
Wrestling feels a lot like making love.

Why did Jacob wrestle with God, why did the others talk?
God surely enjoyed that all-night fling with Jacob:
Told him he'd won,
Renamed him and us the Godwrestler,
Even left him a limp to be sure he'd remember it all.
But ever since, we've talked.
Did something peculiar happen that night?
Did somebody say next day we shouldn't wrestle? Who?

We should wrestle again with our Comrade sometime soon.
Wrestling feels a lot like making love.

But Esau struggled to his feet from his own Wrestle,
And gasped across the river to his brother:
It also
Feels
A lot
Like
Making
War.

—Arthur I. Waskow, *Godwrestling*, pp. 1-2

JOB'S COMPLAINT TO GOD

*So Satan went out from the presence of the L*ord*, and inflicted loathsome sores on Job from the sole of his foot to the crown of his head. Job took a potsherd with which to scrape himself, and sat among the ashes.*

Then his wife said to him, "Do you still persist in your integrity? Curse God, and die." But he said to her, "You speak as any foolish woman would speak. Shall we receive the good at the hand of God, and not receive the bad?" In all this Job did not sin with his lips.

—Job 2:7-10, NRSV

After this, Job opened his mouth and cursed the day of his birth. Job said:

"Let the day perish in which I was born,
and the night that said
'A man-child is conceived.'
Let that day be darkness!
May God above not seek it,
or light shine on it.
Let gloom and deep darkness claim it.
Let clouds settle upon it;
let the blackness of the day terrify it. . . .
Why did I not die at birth,
come forth from the womb and expire?
Why were there knees to receive me,
or breasts for me to suck?
Now I would be lying down and quiet;
I would be asleep; then I would be at rest. . . ."

—Job 3:1-5, 11-13, NRSV

141

"I loathe my life.
I will give free utterance to my complaint;
I will speak in the bitterness of my soul.
I will say to God, Do not condemn me;
let me know why you contend against me.
Does it seem good to you to oppress,
to despise the work of your hands
and favor the schemes of the wicked? . . .
Your hands fashioned and made me;
and now you turn and destroy me.
Remember that you fashioned me like clay;
and will you turn me to dust again? . . .
If I am wicked, woe to me!
If I am righteous, I cannot lift up my head,
for I am filled with disgrace
and look upon my affliction.
Bold as a lion you hunt me;
you repeat your exploits against me.
You renew your witness against me,
and increase your vexation toward me;
you bring fresh troops against me.

Why did you bring me forth from the womb?
Would that I had died before any eye had seen me,
and were as though I had not been,
carried from the womb to the grave.
Are not the days of my life few?
Let me alone, that I may find a little comfort
before I go, never to return,
to the land of gloom and deep darkness,
the land of gloom and chaos,
where light is like darkness."

—Job 10:1-3, 8-9, 15-22, NRSV

JEREMIAH'S CHALLENGE

O Lord, you have enticed me,
*   and I was enticed;*
you have overpowered me,
*   and you have prevailed.*
I have become a laughingstock all day long;
*   everyone mocks me.*
For whenever I speak, I must cry out,
*   I must shout, "Violence and destruction!"*
For the word of the Lord has become for me
*   a reproach and derision all day long.*
If I say, "I will not mention him,
*   or speak any more in his name,"*
then within me there is
*   something like a burning fire shut up in my bones;*
I am weary with holding it in,
*   and I cannot. . . .*

Sing to the Lord;
*   praise the Lord!*
For he has delivered the life of the needy
*   from the hands of evildoers.*

Cursed be the day
*   on which I was born!*
The day when my mother bore me,
*   let it not be blessed!*

Cursed be the man
*   who brought the news to my father, saying,*
"A child is born to you, a son,"
*   making him very glad. . . .*

Why did I come forth from the womb
*   to see toil and sorrow,*
*   and spend my days in shame?*

—Jeremiah 20:7-9, 13-15, 18, NRSV

O Lord, you know;
*   remember me and visit me,*
*   and bring down retribution for me on my persecutors.*
In your forbearance do not take me away;
*   know that on your account I suffer insult.*
Your words were found, and I ate them,
*   and your words became to me a joy*
*   and the delight of my heart;*
for I am called by your name. . . .
Why is my pain unceasing,
*   my wound incurable,*
*   refusing to be healed?*
Truly, you are to me like a deceitful brook,
*   like waters that fail.*

—Jeremiah 15:15-16, 18, NRSV

HANNAH'S STORY

There was a certain man . . . whose name was Elkanah. . . . He had two wives; the name of the one was Hannah, and the name of the other Peninnah. Peninnah had children, but Hannah had no children.

Now this man used to go up year by year from his town to worship and to sacrifice to the Lord *of hosts at Shiloh. . . . On the day when Elkanah sacrificed, he would give portions to his wife Peninnah and to all her sons and daughters, but to Hannah he gave a double portion, because he loved her, though the* Lord *had closed her womb. Her rival used to provoke her severely, to irritate her, because the* Lord *had closed her womb. So it went on year by year; as often as she went up to the house of the* Lord, *she used to provoke her. Therefore Hannah wept and would not eat. Her husband Elkanah said to her, "Hannah, why do you weep? Why do you not eat? Why is your heart sad? Am I not more to you than ten sons?"*

After they had eaten and drunk at Shiloh, Hannah rose and presented herself before the Lord. *Now Eli the priest was sitting on the seat beside the doorpost of the temple of the* Lord. *She was deeply distressed and prayed to the* Lord, *and wept bitterly. She made this vow: "O* Lord *of hosts, if only you will look on the misery of your servant, and remember me, and not forget your servant, but will give to your servant a male child, then I will set him before you as a nazirite until the day of his death. He shall drink neither wine or intoxicants, and no razor shall touch his head."*

As she continued praying before the Lord, *Eli observed her mouth. Hannah was praying silently; only her lips moved, but her voice was not heard; therefore Eli thought she was drunk. So Eli said to her, "How long will you make a drunken spectacle of yourself? Put away your wine." But Hannah answered, "No, my lord, I am a woman deeply troubled; I have drunk neither wine nor strong drink, but I have been pouring out my soul before the* Lord. *Do not regard your servant as a worthless woman, for I have been speaking out of my great anxiety and vexation all this time." Then Eli answered, "Go in peace; the God of Israel grant the petition you have made to him." And she said, "Let your servant find favor in your sight." Then the woman went to her quarters, ate and drank with her husband, and her countenance was sad no longer.*

143   —1 Samuel 1:1-18, NRSV

Woman Weeping

—Vincent Van Gogh

COMPASSION FOR GOD

Abraham Heschel reveals an aspect of spirituality in his discussion of the Kotzker that seems practically absent in Christian life and certainly has never been stressed in my life. It is the aspect of protest against God. He writes: "The refusal to accept the harshness of God's ways in the name of his love was an authentic form of prayer. Indeed, the ancient Prophets of Israel were not in the habit of consenting to God's harsh judgment and did not simply nod, saying, 'Thy will be done.' They often challenged him, as if to say, 'Thy will be changed.' They had often countered and even annulled divine decrees. . . . A man who lived by honesty could not be expected to suppress his anxiety when tormented by profound perplexity. He had to speak out audaciously. Man should never capitulate, even to the Lord. . . . There are some forms of suffering that a man must accept with love and bear in silence. There are other agonies to which he must say no."

This attitude shows, in fact, how close the Jew, who can protest against God, feels to God. When I can only relate to God in terms of submission, I am much more distant from him than when I can question his decrees. Most remarkable, therefore, is that this intimacy with God leads to a feeling that has never been part of my thinking but might be very important: Compassion for God.

Heschel tells the beautiful story of the Polish Jew who stopped praying "because of what happened in Auschwitz." Later, however, he started to pray again. When asked, "What made you change your mind?" he answered, "It suddenly dawned upon me to think how lonely God must be; look with whom he is left. I felt sorry for him."

This attitude brings God and his people very close to each other, so that God is known by his people as the one who suffers with them.

Heschel writes: "The cardinal issue, Why does the God of justice and compassion permit evil to persist? is bound up with the problem of how man should aid God so that his justice and compassion prevail." The most powerful sentence of Heschel is: "Faith is the beginning of compassion, of compassion for God. It is when bursting with God's sights that we are touched by the awareness that beyond all absurdity there is meaning, truth, and love." This is an experience of deep mysticism in which active protest and passive surrender are both present, and man struggles with God as Jacob wrestled with the angel.

—Henri Nouwen, *The Genesee Diary*, pp. 121-122

An old man said: Constant prayer quickly straightens out our thoughts.

—Yushi Nomura, *Desert Wisdom: Sayings from the Desert Fathers*, p. 32

He came out and went, as was his custom, to the Mount of Olives; and the disciples followed him. When he reached the place, he said to them, "Pray that you may not come into the time of trial." Then he withdrew from them about a stone's throw, knelt down, and prayed, "Father, if you are willing, remove this cup from me; yet not my will but yours be done." Then an angel from heaven appeared to him and gave him strength. In his anguish he prayed more earnestly, and his sweat became like great drops of blood falling down on the ground.

—Luke 22:39-44, NRSV

Our Lord in the Garden of Olives

—Rembrandt

MY GOD, MY GOD

My God, my God, why abandon me?
  My groaning words do not help me at all!
All day I call, but you do not answer;
  All night, but I find no rest.
And yet, my God, you are holy,
  Enthroned on Israel's praises.
Our ancestors put their faith in you;
  They had faith, and you rescued them.
They cried out to you and were saved;
  They had faith, and you did not shame them.
But I am a worm, not human at all;
  A disgrace to everyone, scorned by the people.
And all who see me mock me—
  Making faces and shaking their heads:
"You trust in the Lord—let the Lord come to help you;
  Let God be your savior, if God is your friend!"
It was you who drew me out of the womb,
  Who kept me safe on my mother's breast.
I was thrown on you from birth;
  From my mother's womb you have been my God.
Do not be far away from me!
  For trouble is near; there is no one to help. . . .
O Lord, do not be far away;
  Hurry to help me, for you are my strength! . . .

I declare your name to my brothers and sisters;
  In the congregation I praise you:
"All who worship the Lord, . . .
  Now honor and fear your God!
For God will not ignore the poor,
  Nor despise them because they are wretched.
God's face is not hidden from them;
  God hears their cry for help."

—Psalm 22:1-11, 19, 22, 24, *The Psalms: A New Translation for
Prayer and Worship*, translated by Gary Chamberlain,
© 1984, The Upper Room. Used by permission.

*When it was noon, darkness came over the whole land until three
in the afternoon. At three o'clock Jesus cried out with a loud voice,
"Eloi, Eloi, lema sabachthani?" which means, "My God, my God,
why have you forsaken me?" When some of the bystanders heard
it, they said, "Listen, he is calling for Elijah." And someone ran,
filled a sponge with sour wine, put it on a stick, and gave it to him
to drink, saying, "Wait, let us see whether Elijah will come to take
him down." Then Jesus gave a loud cry and breathed his last.*

—Mark 15:33-37, NRSV

LOVE LETTER

I hate you, God.
Love, Madeleine.
> *I write my message on water*
> *and at bedtime I tiptoe upstairs*
> *and let it flow under your door.*

When I am angry with you
I know that you are there
even if you do not answer my knock
even when your butler opens the door an inch
and flaps his thousand wings in annoyance
at such untoward interruption
and says that the master is not at home.
> *I love you, Madeleine.*
> *Hate, God.*

(This is how I treat my friends, he said to one great saint.
No wonder you have so few of them, Lord, she replied.)
> *I cannot turn the other cheek.*
> *It takes all the strength I have*
> *to keep my fist from hitting back*
> *the soldiers shot the baby*
> *the little boys trample the old woman*
> *the gutters are filled with groans*
> *while pleasure seekers knock each other down*
> *in order to get their tickets stamped first.*

I'm turning in my ticket
and my letter of introduction.

You're supposed to do the knocking. Why do you burst my heart?
> *How can I write you*
> *to tell you that I'm angry*
> *when I've been given the wrong address*
> *and I don't even know your real name?*

I take hammer and nails
and tack my message on two crossed pieces of wood:
> *Dear God*
> *is it too much to ask you*
> *to bother to be?*
> *Just show your hindquarters*
> *and let me hear you roar.*

Love,
Madeleine.

—Madeleine L'Engle, *The Weather of the Heart*, pp. 84-85

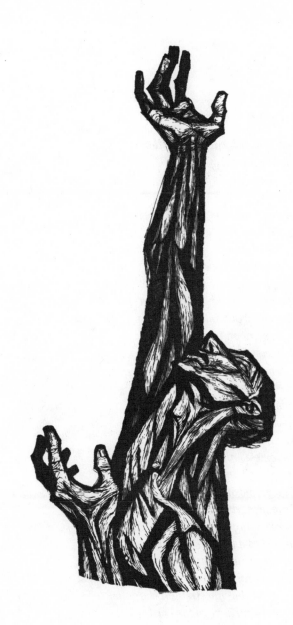

Reach

—Robert Hodgell

DELIVERANCE

I am the man who has known affliction,
    I have felt the rod of his wrath.
It was I whom he led away and left to walk in darkness,
    where no light is.
Against me alone he has turned his hand,
    and so it is all day long.
He has wasted away my flesh and my skin
    and broken all my bones. . . .
He has walled me in so that I cannot escape,
    and weighed me down with fetters;
even when I cry out and call for help,
    he rejects my prayer. . . .
He lies in wait for me like a bear
    or a lion lurking in a covert. . . .
    He has strung his bow
and made me the target for his arrows;
he has pierced my kidneys with shafts
    drawn from his quiver.
I have become a laughing-stock to all nations,
    the target of their mocking songs all day.
He has given me my fill of bitter herbs
    and made me drunk with wormwood.
He has broken my teeth on gravel;
    fed on ashes, I am racked with pain;
peace has gone out of my life,
    and I have forgotten what prosperity means.
Then I cry out that my strength has gone
    and so has my hope in the Lord.

The memory of my distress and my wanderings
    is wormwood and gall.
    Remember, O remember,
    and stoop down to me.
All this I take to heart
    and therefore I will wait patiently:
the Lord's true love is surely not spent,
    nor his compassion failed;
    they are new every morning,
    so great is his constancy.
The Lord, I say, is all that I have;
    therefore I will wait for him patiently.
The Lord is good to those who look for him,
    to all who seek him;
it is good to wait in patience and sigh
    for deliverance by the Lord.

—Lamentations 3:1-4, 7-8, 10, 12-26, NEB

WHAT A FRIEND WE HAVE IN JESUS

What a Friend we have in Jesus,
All our sins and griefs to bear!
What a privilege to carry
Everything to God in prayer!
O what peace we often forfeit,
O what needless pain we bear,
All because we do not carry
Everything to God in prayer!

Have we trials and temptations?
Is there trouble anywhere?
We should never be discouraged;
Take it to the Lord in prayer!
Can we find a friend so faithful,
Who will all our sorrows share?
Jesus knows our every weakness;
Take it to the Lord in prayer.

Are we weak and heavy laden,
Cumbered with a load of care?
Precious Savior, still our refuge!
Take it to the Lord in prayer!
Do thy friends despise, forsake thee?
Take it to the Lord in prayer!
In His arms He'll take and shield thee;
Thou wilt find a solace there.

—Joseph M. Scriven, 1819-1886

EXERCISES

In Session

1. Talk with the person you spoke with last week about your success in practicing the discipline you outlined for yourself. Then take some time to revise your discipline to something you believe you can do for one whole month.
2. Write a psalm of complaint, completing the statement: "Why, O God, _____?"
3. Discuss the whole experience of wrestling with God. Have you ever been angry or disappointed with God? What did you do about it? Do you agree that loving God demands we give God *everything* in our minds and hearts?

    Your wrestling with God may not be out of anger or disappointment, but more a struggle with a decision in your life, or with what to do about a relationship, a difficult situation in your family, in your church, or in society. It may come in a time of confusion or anxiety. Include this aspect of wrestling in your discussion.

At Home

1. Commit yourself to practicing your (revised) prayer discipline for one full month. This will give you enough time to adequately evaluate your discipline and to determine what revisions need to be made. Use your journal to record your reactions.
2. As usual, read Reflections and Windows (chapter 7) for ten minutes each day.

8

CHAPTER 8

PRAYER
AND JUSTICE/
COMPASSION

Mercy and faithfulness have met;
justice and peace have embraced.
Faithfulness shall spring from the earth
and justice look down from heaven.

—Psalm 85:10-11, *A New Translation*

What does God require of you
in this commandment [the eighth]?

That I do whatever I can
    for my neighbor's good,
that I treat him
    as I would like others to treat me,
and that I work faithfully
    so that I may share with those in need.

—Heidelberg Catechism, Q & A 111

*Jesus Christ
Driving Out
the Money
Changers*

—Rembrandt

155

REFLECTION

The spiritual life is not hidden inside us. It's practical—it affects everything we say and do. Living in the presence of God, being in touch with God's Spirit, being fine-tuned to God's sensitivities involves us in reflecting God's concerns for all people, resonating God's moral tone for the world, embodying God's will through our living. In fact, the Old and New Testaments indicate that you can tell a person's relationship with God by looking at his or her relationship with other people.

Is not this what I require of you as a fast:
to loose the fetters of injustice,
to untie the knots of the yoke,
to snap every yoke
and set free those who have been crushed?
Is it not sharing your food with the hungry,
taking the homeless poor into your house,
clothing the naked when you meet them
and never evading a duty to your kinsfolk?
Then shall your light break forth like the dawn
and soon you will grow healthy like a wound newly
healed;
your own righteousness shall be your vanguard
and the glory of the Lord your rearguard.
Then, if you call, the Lord will answer;
if you cry to him, the answer will be: "Here I am."

If you cease to pervert justice,
to point the accusing finger and lay false charges,
if you feed the hungry from your own plenty
and satisfy the needs of the wretched,
then your light will rise like dawn out of darkness
and your dusk be like noonday;
the Lord will be your guide continually
and will satisfy your needs in the shimmering heat;
he will give you strength of limb;
you will be like a well-watered garden,
like a spring whose waters never fail.

—Isaiah 58:6-11, NEB

I hate, I spurn your pilgrim-feasts;
I will not delight in your sacred ceremonies.
When you present your sacrifices and offerings
I will not accept them,
nor look on the buffaloes of your shared-offerings.
Spare me the sound of your songs;
I cannot endure the music of your lutes.
Let justice roll on like a river
and righteousness like an ever-flowing stream.

—Amos 5:21-24, NEB

Jesus shocks us as we are about to come before God with gestures of gratitude, or are about to kneel for prayer:

> *So when you are offering your gift at the altar, if you remember that your brother or sister has something against you, leave your gift there before the altar and go; first be reconciled to your brother or sister, and then come and offer your gift.*
>
> —Matthew 5:23-24, NRSV

Jesus suggests that giving gifts to God—even money, even hymns and worship, even coming to the sacrament, even prayers—is *offensive* to the divine majesty unless they are expressions of *just human relationships.* Jesus urges us not to offer anything to God until we have been reconciled with our brother—who includes sister, parent, child, spouse, neighbor, enemy, friend, foreigner, black, white, red, and yellow; the hungry, the poor, the widowed and the orphan, the sick and the oppressed. Do any of these have something against you? Then go first to them and be reconciled before you offer your prayer.

Who of us would ever get back to prayer and worship and offering if we obeyed this command?

I mentioned to someone that I was going to speak about this text in my church on a Sunday, and she asked: "What do you want to do, empty out your church?"

Is it that obvious that we have so much reconciliation, so much peacemaking, so much justice-doing, so much conflict-resolving to do?

Prayer and the spiritual life, you see, are not an escape from life but a confrontation with life. "True spirituality is not a leisure-time activity, a diversion from life. It is essentially subversive, and the test of its genuineness is practical."[1] A zealous involvement with "holy things" can never be a way of avoiding the pain that prevails in the world or the alienation that exists between ourselves and a brother or sister. When such conflict or grievance prevails, we are clearly to leave our sacramental or gratitude gifts behind and make things right that are now wrong.[2]

Jesus spoke of grievances others have against us—not those we have against others. That's not to say that grudges against others are healthy. They interfere with our relationship with the God who tells us to love our enemies. In fact, the Bible tells us that long-lived anger— the kind we brood over, the kind that seeks revenge (Matt. 5:21-22)—is as bad as murder. Anger separates us from people. Gratitude unites us. But in a real sense Jesus does not mention our grievances against others because he presupposes we will not have any enemies, that we are a people who love others, even our "enemies."

So Jesus says, "If there are any people who have a grievance *against you,*" who have cause to be angry with *you,* then reconciliation is necessary. Think of what needs reconciling in your life—with parents, children, brothers or sisters, your spouse or friend, professor or student, a boss or employee. Who would get back to prayers if we had to clear up all those relationships first? Yet that's exactly what Jesus tells us to do.

Or think of our nation. We are well aware that millions of Americans live in poverty. We know that the economic gap between whites and minorities hasn't disappeared and that structural unemployment hits minorities with devastating force. We see that racism and sexism still exist in society, alienating people from each other. Because of these problems, people in our own country, schools, or even churches may have something against us. And it doesn't stop there. People in countries around the world are being treated unjustly and, as a result, may have something against us.

Do we hear these concerns as we go to prayer and worship? As we give our gifts, do we stop to think of those who may have few monetary gifts to bring? Do we hear the cries for just human relationships?

Christian spirituality is the spirituality of the Poor Man of Nazareth who took upon himself the form of a Servant. To know God is to do justice and plead the cause of the oppressed; to know God in Christ is to share in his work of establishing justice in the earth, and to share in his poverty and oppression. . . . God in Christ becomes poor and oppressed, making himself one with all the poor and oppressed peoples of the earth. . . . To follow the way of the Kingdom is therefore to follow him who fed the hungry, healed the sick, befriended the outcast, and blessed the peacemakers.[3]

If we pray "in his spirit" we can afford to be despised by those who consider themselves to be intelligent and enlightened; but not by those who are disconsolate, suffering or oppressed.[4]

Prayer presupposes justice.

Prayer presupposes as well as leads us to our relationship with God. We belong to God, are addressed by God, and in turn address God. An audacious idea! We belong to God with our whole being, and that includes all our relationships—political, economic, and social—with all kinds of people. In fact, we belong to God *along with* all other image-bearers of God. When we pray to our heavenly Parent, as the Lord's Prayer has us pray, we are praying together with all the children of God.

Can we pray that way if we do not hear what justice and compassion mean for someone different from us—someone Black, or Hispanic, or white, or poor, or less educated, or female, or male, or Russian, or Chinese or . . . Do we hear the prayers of others offered alongside our prayers? Do we hear their anguish, their rage, their hopes? Do we pray *with* them as well as *for* them?

Put bluntly: a church, a Christian community, a believer, that is exclusive in attitude or practice along racial, social class, gender, age, or any other human lines can offer only partial, distorted prayers, only tainted gifts.

If any of those other images of God have anything against you, leave your offerings and go be reconciled! The concern of justice is not something removed from us as we pray. We are not separate from others who suffer, but we *suffer with* (com-passion) broken people of the world. *Obedience* means we "hear" (ob-audire)—not only hear God but also hear the cries of the suffering, the people who need their due (justice). Compassion involves us in a deep consciousness of our solidarity with all people rather than our distinction from them. It involves us in responding, almost automatically and naturally, in service to people in need; doing actions we may never have dreamed of.

This story is told of Abba Agathon, a monk of the Egyptian desert in the third century:

Going to town one day to sell some small articles, Abba Agathon met a cripple on the roadside, paralyzed in his legs, who asked him where he was going. Abba Agathon replied, "To town, to sell some things." The other said, "Do me the favor of carrying me there." So he carried him to the town. The cripple said to him, "Put me down where you sell your wares." He did so. When he had sold an article, the cripple asked, "What did you sell it for?" and he told him the price. The other said, "Buy me a cake," and he bought it. When Abba Agathon had sold a second article, the sick man asked, "How much did you sell it for?" And he told him the price of it. Then the other said, "Buy me this," and he bought it. When Agathon, having sold all his wares, wanted to go, he said to him, "Are you going back?" and he replied, "Yes." Then said he, "Do me the favor of carrying me back to the place where you found me." Once more picking him up, he carried him back to that place. Then the cripple said, "Agathon, you are filled with divine blessings in heaven and on earth." Raising his eyes, Agathon saw no man; it was an angel of the Lord come to try him.[5]

With what ease the desert monk responds to the disabled man! No questions, no diagnoses, no bargaining, no calling in a specialized agency. He just does what is asked. He carries the man. Serves him. Cares for him. Acts in solidarity with him. Has compassion. He answers the cry he has heard. He obeys. He said at another time: "If I could meet a leper, give him my body and take his, I should be very happy."[6] Agathon could go to prayers knowing that no one had anything against him.

Prayer presupposes justice and compassion.

But justice and compassion also presuppose prayer. I imagine that monk heard the cry of the disabled man almost automatically because he had heard the cry many times before—in prayer. Did you notice how silent Agathon was? He said practically nothing. Part of the discipline of being a monk in the desert was to be silent, in solitude, in order to listen in prayer. In prayer, Agathon was in the presence of God—silent. The God to whom nothing human is alien; the God who fully experienced the brokenness of our human condition. Agathon could care because he knew the God who cares.

The God to whom he prayed (and to whom we must pray) is revealed in Jesus Christ, who joined us in our suffering. He became "inghettoed" in our human situation, identified with our destiny, was vulnerable to the wounds of our suffering-prone humanity.[7] In Jesus, God experienced our suffering from inside, manifesting the depths of divine compassion.

The Gospels express this poignantly when they record that Jesus was "moved with compassion" (Mark 1:41, for example). He was moved in his *splagchna,* entrails, guts—"the place where our most intimate and intense emotions are located." How deep and mysterious this expression is. "The compassion Jesus felt was obviously quite different from superficial or passing feelings of sorrow or sympathy. It extended to the most vulnerable part of his being." We get a more expressive image with an "old Hebrew word for com-passion, *rachamim,* which refers to the womb of Yahweh. Compassion is such a deep, central, and powerful emotion in Jesus that it can be described as a movement of the womb of God. When Jesus was moved with compassion, the source of all" that lives "trembled, the ground of all love" and gentleness "burst open, and the depth of God's immense, inexhaustible and unfathomable tenderness revealed itself."[8] For Christ compassion involved identification with us: emptying himself and becoming like us; taking human form, the condition of a servant. Compassion meant obedience, hearing (cf. Phil. 2:5-11). Solidarity and servanthood were not just techniques to get something done; they were the results of obedience. They came from listening to and responding to God's love, from closeness to God.[9]

Prayer opens us to a closeness with God, the compassionate God we know in Jesus Christ. And the closer we get to God, the closer we get to the people of the world. We find the world at the heart of God. A disciple of Christ does not avoid the pain of the world, but penetrates into its center. The deeper the prayer is, the deeper we enter into solidarity with a suffering world. In solitude this compassionate solidarity grows. In solitude we realize that the roots of all conflict, war, injustice, cruelty, hatred, jealousy, and envy are deeply anchored in our own hearts. Nothing human is alien to us either. In prayer we assume responsibility for injustice in our self and in the world. Thomas Merton implies that

> *such awareness and action are tied together; whoever attempts to act and do things for others or for the world without deepening their own self-understanding, freedom, integrity and capacity to love, will not have anything to give others. They will communicate to others nothing but the contagion of their own obsession, their aggressivity, their ego-centered ambitions.*[10]

He even goes on to say that work for others that does not lead to deeper purity of heart is little more than the imposition of our own compulsiveness on our society.

Prayer helps us get in touch with God and with ourselves and makes us aware of others. We find others before God in their need, just as we are there before God in our need. "Intercessory prayer" becomes bringing people to God or joining people before God. We *suffer with* God in Christ for the salvation of the world, for freedom for the oppressed, for the cessation of war, for the healing of sickness, for the comfort of the anxious and sorrowing. In prayer, we gradually identify with the people for whom we pray as we bring them to the care of God. We hear people there! That is why I said that Agathon probably heard the cry of the lame man long before he met the man on the road. He heard it in prayer. So when he heard it again he responded with action he never dreamed of. But he did it quite naturally. The act of praying for someone commits us to working in other ways for that person or situation. "To clasp the hands in prayer is the beginning of an uprising against the disorder of the world."[11] Prayer is one way we are actively engaged in changing the world.

> *The contemplative who can stand back from a situation and see it for what it is is more threatening to an unjust social system than the frenzied activist who is so involved in the situation that he cannot see clearly at all.*[12]

Thus, we do not stop prayer or worship, even though justice is not accomplished and our compassion is incomplete and all relationships are not healed. In fact, we recognize not only that our just relationships are needed for communion with God but also that communion with God is necessary for establishing such relationships. Before God we not only offer prayers of intercession but prayers of confession. We admit that we are broken, incomplete, unjust. We know that it will take some *divine* working in our lives and in the world to establish justice. We admit our failure, but we also admit that God is still at work accepting us and others into the divine family, restoring us to the image of God, removing grudges between images of God, breaking down walls between hostile people, bringing about reconciliation, justice, peace, and compassion.

Prayer aims at opening ourselves to a relationship with that God; worship celebrates the possibility and actuality of getting close to God and God to us, and thus the possibility of removing barriers. Our work for just human relationships needs that relationship to God. Thus our concern for justice and compassion leads us back to prayer.

And the life of prayer once again certainly leads us back to life in the world. "It is not those who say to me 'Lord, Lord,' who will enter the kingdom of heaven, but the person who does the will of my Father in heaven" (Matt. 7:21-22, The Jerusalem Bible). We are full circle, arriving where we began. The final criterion of the spiritual life is not prayer but action (Matt. 25:31-46). Prayer urges us to aggressively serve God and those people whose cry we hear. It urges us to actions we never imagined—actions that make visible God's boundless compassion or justice—but which seem as natural to us as they did to Agathon.

So we dare pray even when the social task remains incomplete and fragmented. For prayer can help us hear the cries more distinctly, can help us see the task more clearly, can help us relate to divine justice more challengingly. Justice and compassion presuppose prayer. And prayer presupposes justice and compassion. Prayer may never be mere speech (silence) unaccompanied by the transformation of the one who prays. Prayer needs to carry with it the commitment of our whole being to bring about the just conditions that make prayer possible; prayer must have the inner intentionality of being more firmly related to the divine and more reflective of the divine desire for justice in our relationships with others.

Prayer and justice/compassion presuppose each other. We need to do both without ceasing![13]

FOOTNOTES

1. Leech, *True Prayer, An Invitation to Christian Spirituality*, 79.
2. Buteyn, "Spirituality, Piety and Conflict" in the *Pacific Theological Review*, Fall, 1981, 10.
3. Leech, 73.
4. Metz and Rahner, *The Courage to Pray*, 20.
5. *The Sayings of the Desert Fathers*, trs. Benedicta Ward, 21-22.
6. *The Sayings of the Desert Fathers*, 20.
7. Smedes, "Suffering: The Christian Style of Life," *The Reformed Journal*, February 1969, 12.
8. McNeill, Morrison, Nouwen, *Compassion*, 16.
9. McNeill, Morrison, Nouwen, *Compassion*. The book is devoted in part to developing the concept of compassion as solidarity, servanthood, and obedience.
10. Edwards, *Living Simply through the Day*, 163-164.
11. Karl Barth, quoted by Leech, 68.
12. Leech, 85.
13. I am grateful to Dr. John Gunneman for some of the thoughts in this chapter, which he developed in a moving Lenten sermon given in Yale Divinity School chapel in 1980.

WINDOWS
TO INSIGHT

The more I think it over, the more I feel that there is noth-ing more truly artistic than to love people.

—Vincent Van Gogh

The Good Samartian

—Rembrandt

SELF-EMPTYING

If then there is any encouragement in Christ, any consolation from love, any sharing in the Spirit, any compassion and sympathy, make my joy complete; be of the same mind, having the same love, being in full accord and of one mind. Do nothing from selfish ambition or conceit, but in humility regard others as better than yourselves. Let each of you look not to your own interests, but to the interests of others. Let the same mind be in you that was in Christ Jesus,

> *who, though he was in the form of God*
>> *did not regard equality with God*
>> *as something to be exploited,*
> *but emptied himself,*
>> *taking the form of a slave,*
>> *being born in human likeness.*
> *And being found in human form*
>> *he humbled himself*
>> *and became obedient to the point of death—*
>> *even death on a cross.*

> *Therefore God also highly exalted him*
>> *and gave him the name*
>> *that is above every name,*
> *so that at the name of Jesus*
>> *every knee should bend,*
>> *in heaven and on earth and under the earth,*
> *and every tongue should confess*
>> *that Jesus Christ is Lord,*
>> *to the glory of God the Father.*

—Philippians 2:1-11, NRSV

O MASTER, LET ME WALK WITH THEE

O Master, let me walk with Thee
In lowly paths of service free;
Tell me Thy secret, help me bear
The strain of toil, the fret of care.

Help me the slow of heart to move
By some clear winning word of love;
Teach me the wayward feet to stay,
And guide them in the homeward way.

Teach me Thy patience; still with Thee
In closer, dearer company,
In work that keeps faith sweet and strong,
In trust that triumphs over wrong.

In hope that sends a shining ray
Far down the future's broadening way,
In peace that only Thou canst give,
With Thee, O Master, let me live.

—Washington Gladden, 1836-1908

COMPASSION AND THE CONTEMPLATIVE LIFE

Monday, 23

Often I have said to people, "I will pray for you," but how often did I really enter into the full reality of what that means? I now see how indeed I can enter deeply into the other and pray to God from his center. When I really bring my friends and the many I pray for into my innermost being and feel their pains, their struggles, their cries in my own soul, then I leave myself, so to speak, and become them, then I have compassion. Compassion lies at the heart of our prayer for our fellow human beings. When I pray for the world, I become the world; when I pray for the endless needs of the millions, my soul expands and wants to embrace them all and bring them into the presence of God. But in the midst of that experience I realize that compassion is not mine but God's gift to me. I cannot embrace the world, but God can. I cannot pray, but God can pray in me. When God became as we are, that is, when God allowed all of us to enter into his intimate life, it became possible for us to share in his infinite compassion.

In praying for others, I lose myself and become the other, only to be found by the divine love which holds the whole of humanity in a compassionate embrace.

Tuesday, 24

Yesterday I shared with John Eudes some of my thoughts about prayer for others. He not only confirmed my thoughts but also led me further by saying that compassion belongs to the center of the contemplative life. When we become the other and so enter into the presence of God, then we are true contemplatives. True contemplatives, then, are not the ones who withdrew from the world to save their own soul, but the ones who enter into the center of the world and pray to God from there.

—Henri Nouwen, *The Genesee Diary*, p. 123

Abba Epiphanus said: God sells righteousness very cheap to those who are eager to buy: namely, for a little piece of bread, worthless clothes, a cup of cold water and one coin.

—Yushi Nomura, *Desert Wisdom: Sayings from the Desert Fathers*, p. 101

BLESS US

God be gracious to us and bless us,
God make his face shine upon us,
*   that his ways may be known on earth*
*   and his saving power among all the nations.*

Let the peoples praise thee, O God;
*   let all peoples praise thee.*
Let all nations rejoice and shout in triumph;
*   for thou dost judge the peoples with justice*
*   and guidest the nations of the earth.*

Let the peoples praise thee, O God;
*   let all peoples praise thee.*
The earth has given its increase
*   and God, our God, will bless us.*

God grant us his blessing
that all the ends of the earth may fear him.

—Psalm 67, NEB

JUSTICE AND PEACE

I will hear what the Lord God has to say,
a voice that speaks of peace,
*   peace for his people and his friends*
and those who turn to him in their hearts.
His help is near for those who fear him
and his glory will dwell in our land.

Mercy and faithfulness have met;
justice and peace have embraced.
Faithfulness shall spring from the earth
and justice look down from heaven.

The Lord will make us prosper
and our earth shall yield its fruit.
Justice shall march before him
and peace shall follow his steps.

—Psalm 85:8-13, *A New Translation*

Jesus Christ Healing the Sick (commonly known as "The Hundred Guilder Print")

—Rembrandt

167

PRAYER AND POLITICS

If we are to pray in the spirit of Christ, we cannot turn our backs on the sufferings of others. Prayer demands that we love our fellow humans; we have no choice. It can make prayer extremely dangerous, for example, in situations where humanity is systematically suppressed and people are forced to live as though no bonds of allegiance existed between them. This need for humanity urges Christians today to adopt a positive attitude towards prayer. We must pray not just for the poor and unfortunate but with them. This contradicts our instinctive tendency to avoid the company of those who are unhappy or suffering. If we pray "in his spirit" we can afford to be despised by those who consider themselves to be intelligent and enlightened; but not by those who are disconsolate, suffering or oppressed. And this means that prayer is of necessity political and influential. . . .

Hence we must take care not to let our prayers turn into a eulogistic evasion of what really matters, serving merely to lift the apathy from our souls and our indifference and lack of sympathy towards other people's suffering. . . . A mature attitude towards prayer presupposes the readiness to assume responsibility. . . .

The qualities of this liberating, edifying God to whom we pray must be visible in our conduct and attitudes.

—Johann Baptist Metz, *The Courage to Pray,* pp. 19-22

Prayer which does not have direct human and social application is not Christian prayer. . . .

Merton held that solitude and interior prayer were closely linked with the awakening of the social conscience. . . . It is in solitude, in the depths of a person's own aloneness, that there lie the resources for resistance to injustice. . . .

For Merton the understanding of prayer is crucial to the understanding of social change. There is no split between spirituality and social responsibility. "The time will shortly be upon us, if it is not already here, when the pursuit of contemplation becomes a strictly subversive activity" (Daniel Berrigan).

—Kenneth Leech, *True Prayer,* pp. 74, 82-84

*The Christ of
the Breadlines*

—Fritz Eichenberg

169

PRAYER OF THE HEART

A final characteristic of the prayer of the heart is that it includes all our concerns. When we enter with our mind into our heart and there stand in the presence of God, then all our mental preoccupations become prayer. The power of the prayer of the heart is precisely that through it all that is on our mind becomes prayer.

When we say to people, "I will pray for you," we make a very important commitment. The sad thing is that this remark often remains nothing but a well-meant expression of concern. But when we learn to descend with our mind into our heart, then all those who have become part of our lives are led into the healing presence of God and touched by him in the center of our being. We are speaking here about a mystery for which words are inadequate. It is the mystery that the heart, which is the center of our being, is transformed by God into his own heart, a heart large enough to embrace the entire universe. Through prayer we can carry in our heart all human pain and sorrow, all conflicts and agonies, all torture and war, all hunger, loneliness, and misery, not because of some great psychological or emotional capacity, but because God's heart has become one with ours.

Here we catch sight of the meaning of Jesus' words, "Shoulder my yoke and learn from me, for I am gentle and humble in heart,

and you will find rest for your souls. Yes, my yoke is easy and my burden light" (Matt. 11:29-30, JB). Jesus invites us to accept his burden, which is the burden of the whole world, a burden that includes human suffering in all times and places. But this divine burden is light, and we can carry it when our heart has been transformed into the gentle and humble heart of our Lord.

Here we can see the intimate relationship between prayer and ministry. The discipline of leading all our people with their struggles into the gentle and humble heart of God is the discipline of prayer as well as the discipline of ministry. As long as ministry only means that we worry a lot about people and their problems; as long as it means an endless number of activities which we can hardly coordinate, we are still very much dependent on our own narrow and anxious heart. But when our worries are led to the heart of God and there become prayer, then ministry and prayer become two manifestations of the same all-embracing love of God.

—Henri Nouwen, *The Way of the Heart*, pp. 87-88

THE PRAYER OF SAINT FRANCIS

Lord, make me an instrument of thy peace.
Where there is hatred, let me sow love;
Where there is injury, pardon;
Where there is doubt, faith;
Where there is despair, hope;
Where there is darkness, light;
Where there is sadness, joy.

O Divine Master, grant that I may not so much seek
To be consoled, as to console;
Not so much to be understood as to understand;
Not so much to be loved as to love;
For it is in giving that we receive;
It is in pardoning that we are pardoned;
It is in dying that we awaken to eternal life.

TRANSFORMED VISION

Is the Christian life of prayer simply an evasion of the problems and anxieties of contemporary existence? . . . If we pray "in the Spirit" we are certainly not running away from life, negating visible reality in order to "see God." For "the Spirit of the Lord has filled the whole earth." Prayer does not blind us to the world, but it transforms our vision of the world, and makes us see it, all people, and all the history of humankind, in the light of God.

—Thomas Merton, *The Climate of Monastic Prayer,* p. 149

I feel that my work lies in the heart of the people, that I must keep close to the ground, that I must grasp life in its depths, and make progress through many cares and troubles.

—Vincent Van Gogh, *The Complete Letters*, 197, I, 365

I have tried to emphasize that those people, eating their potatoes in the lamplight, have dug the earth with those very hands they put in the dish, and so it speaks of manual labor, *and how they have honestly earned their food.*

—Vincent Van Gogh, *The Complete Letters*, 404, II, 370

The Potato Eaters

—Vincent Van Gogh

A SPIRITUALITY OF ACTION

The "center" which we seek in contemplation does not exist as something separate from our physical, emotional and intellectual life. It is our "heart," which in contemplative literature means "the deepest psychological ground of one's personality," and "the root and source of all one's own inner truth." In contemplation, then, we seek to achieve a harmony of the total personality, the integration of thought and action, of what goes on inside us and what we do outwardly. Prayer is never focused exclusively on the inner life; it always flows back again to the external circumstances, events and experience of life. And contemplation affects the way in which we "go back" to those external affairs. Merton writes: "Prayer does not blind us to the world, but it transforms our vision of the world." Every object and act become ultimately significant in relation to the purposes of the God who reveals that history is the context in which we are to forge a truly human existence through acts of love, justice, peace and unity. In biblical religion, spirituality cannot be a strictly private matter or inner experience. Gutierrez writes: "Peace, justice, love and freedom are not private realities; they are not only internal attitudes. They are social realities, implying a historical liberation."

In our model of contemporary spirituality then, the function of contemplation is that of integrating in the deepest levels of our consciousness, our understanding of self and our world in a transformed vision that sees both in relation to the creative and redemptive purpose of God. This insight is born of reflection on the biblical symbols and message, is nurtured by the liturgy and community of the church, and is tested in concrete action in history. In practice, the pattern of this "spirituality of action" may be broken down into separate moments. The contradictions of our humanity in actual experience require analysis, involving all of the available tools of critical inquiry. But, such analysis is not value-free; reason is not mere technical rationality, but the power of truth and justice to transform our historical realities. It is informed by the symbols and concepts of biblical tradition. Meditation on our historical experience takes place in the "heart," in the depths of our personality, where, "in the dominion of the Spirit," we are undergoing the continuous process of transformation. Then, guided by reason, and empowered by contemplation, we return to the arena of experience. The unity of contemplation and action gives us neither perfect wisdom nor perfect action, for our return to the world of action always generates new experience, new contradictions, which will require fresh analysis, new contemplation, new action. But that fits exactly our understanding of our world, and our history, and of Christian praxis as growth in truth through continuing transformation of ourselves and our world.

—Lawrence M. Bouldin, "Contemplation and Action,"
The NICM Journal, pp. 23-25

Peasant Woman Gleaning Grain

—Vincent Van Gogh

EXERCISES

In Session

In Session

Worship together, following this evening prayers format:
Invocation:

Leader: "O God, come to my assistance."
People: "O Lord, make haste to help me."

Psalm: Read Psalm 67 in unison (see Windows).
Sing the Doxology—"Praise God from whom all blessings flow. . . ."

Scripture: (Read aloud by group leader or others)
Philippians 2:1-11 (see Windows)
or
Song of Mary from Luke 1:46-55

Prayer: Silence for reflection on Scripture.
Spoken prayers by group members for others, including:
— family members or friends in need
— someone they don't like or who doesn't like them
— the sick, the poor, the suffering, the hungry, the lonely, etc.
— those in leadership positions in our world
— those most directly affected by current world problems, dangers
The Prayer of St. Francis
(in unison—see page 171)

Hymn: "O Master, Let Me Walk with Thee"
(see p. 163)
or
hymn of your choice

At Home

1. Continue practicing your personal prayer discipline. Please include prayers of justice and compassion in your discipline this week; for instance, one day you might pray for family members, the next day for world events, the next for people at work, and so forth. On Sunday try coming to church a little early and praying for people as they enter the church. (Don't forget the pastor!)

2. Most people read a daily newspaper, watch TV news, or scan a weekly newsmagazine. A simple way to build a habit of societal contemplation is to contemplate the news and pray for the people involved. It takes no longer to pray the news than to read it or watch it (William R. Callahan, *Noisy Contemplation,* p. 20).

3. Try to take ten minutes a day for reading Reflections and Windows of chapter 8.

4. Remember to use your journal for reactions to chapter 8 and to your personal prayer discipline.

9

THE GOAL IS GLORY

What is the chief end of human life?
To know God by whom men were created.

What reason have you for saying so?
Because he created us and placed us in this world to be
glorified by us, and it is indeed right that our life, of
which he himself is the beginning, should be devoted to his glory.

—John Calvin, *The Catechism of the Church of Geneva*

So, whether you eat or drink, or whatever you do, do everything for
the glory of God.

—1 Corinthians 10:31, RSV

What does the first request mean?

Hallowed be thy name *means,*
Help us to really know you,
to bless, worship, and praise you
  for all your works
  and for all that shines forth from them:
    your almighty power, wisdom, kindness,
    justice, mercy, and truth.

—Heidelberg Catechism, Q & A 122

The Starry Night

—Vincent Van Gogh

179

REFLECTION

The spiritual life is living in depth. But its focus is also the highest heights: the glory of God.

> *In all things so act that the glory may be God's through Jesus Christ; to him belong glory and power for ever and ever. Amen.*
>
> —1 Peter 4:11, NEB

People who belong to God recognize how gracious our God is, and how awesomely glorious:

> *I saw the Lord seated on a throne, high and exalted, and the skirt of his robe filled the temple. About him were attendant seraphim, and each had six wings; one pair covered his face and one pair his feet, and one pair was spread in flight. They were calling ceaselessly to one another,*
> *Holy, holy, holy is the Lord of Hosts:*
> *the whole earth is full of his glory.*
> *And, as each one called, the threshold shook to its foundations, while the house was filled with smoke. Then I cried,*
> *Woe is me! I am lost,*
> *for I am a man of unclean lips*
> *and I dwell among a people of unclean lips;*
> *yet with these eyes I have seen the King,*
> *the Lord of Hosts.*
>
> Isaiah 6:1-5, NEB

The glory of God is the active presence of God.

> *Some Bible writers have a habit of talking about Jahweh's coming to the tabernacle or the temple in terms of the "appearance of his glory" (Ex. 40:34; Lev. 9:6; I Kings 8:11; Ezek. 1:28). They mean, of course, that Jahweh Himself appeared. They did not see Him appear materially; but they did see the thrust of His Godness. When it happened, it was so impressive that the writers spoke of it as the coming of a cloud that carried His glory. The temple is not great enough to contain His glory when it comes (1 Kings 8:27). The whole earth is required for it, as the cherubs chant in Isaiah 6:3.*
>
> *The glory of the Lord—this is a way of announcing Jahweh's tremendous "presence" in the midst of Israel. It can suggest His coming there to live. But His glory is revealed, too, in His actions; in what He does for Israel (Ps. 111:2). And what He does is great! Jahweh "glorifies himself" when He liberates Israel from Pharaoh's hands (Ex. 14 4ff.). He "glorifies himself" in His judgment of the sinner who corrupts His handiwork (Lev. 10:3). Sometimes the writers say that Jahweh "sanctifies himself," shows Himself as the Holy One. What this means is that God creates respect for Himself (in the eyes of the peoples and their gods) by performing great deeds of judg-*

ment and liberation (see, e.g., Num. 20:2-13; Ezek. 20:41; 28:22).

The "glory of the Lord" usually calls up the picture of God in action, God as He is in His deeds. Whether it is God's action in nature or in human affairs does not matter for the Israelite; it is still the "Lord's glory."[1]

Being in the dazzling presence of God is a wondrous experience; realizing God's majestic, just, and compassionate action in the world and in our lives urges us to let all thanks break loose![2]

We come so often to God, if we come at all, as beggars. We ask and beg: give me; bless me; help me; guide me; grant me. And that's one necessary level of our existence.

But in thanksgiving and adoration we come to God not to ask but to give! We come not whimpering but shouting praise; not in guilt but in gratitude. We feel not distant from God but close to God. We are like a traveler who is home again at last, the prodigal at a banquet. Those moments may be seldom, but when they happen we know that we were created *for God.*

In a rare moment of happiness,
    when the past does not plague you,
    when the present is serene,
    when the future holds no threats,
    when life is not conditioned by all kinds of ifs,
    when you simply say "Thanks,"
it all comes together for you. Your whole life is focused.

You leave all that held you bound—money and misery, sin and sickness—leave it all behind in doxology. There are only joy and cheers!

You experience that sometimes when you attend sporting events or concerts. All the people, thousands of them with worries about marriages and mortgages, sex and sin, God and gold, are all of one mind, all wrapped up. They become admirers, praise-shouters. That's something of a parable of what the goal of a thankful life is: with one voice people cheering and applauding God.

It took me a long time to like the notion of being a God-glorifier. I didn't like a God who created human beings just to hear their applause. I had a juvenile fantasy of a narcissistic deity, liking what he saw in the mirror, but hungry for rave reviews. The Lord later gave me better insights into the playfulness of being a God-glorifier. One learns theology in many ways. For instance, I went to a concert not long ago to hear a great violinist perform. It was a splendid concert. Afterwards, we in the audience did our own "playing"; we applauded and applauded and applauded. The violinist bowed and left the stage. We would bring him back by applauding and yelling "Bravo!" He would come back, obviously enjoying every decibel, and then retire again. Then we would bring him back with our doxology. He let us play with him. As this game was going on, we were all taken out of ourselves, in a kind of ecstasy, in a game we all played together. And I thought: glorifying God can be a wonderful game to play.[3]

For a moment, for eternity, we forget tears and struggles and all is joy! We know we are created for God!

We know that with certainty in those precious moments when we sing the Doxology with so much inner strength and conviction that we become the choir directors of the universe.

Sing a new song to the Lord;
*   Sing to the Lord, all the world. . . .*
Give to the Lord, you tribes and peoples,
*   Give to the Lord glory and strength.*
Give the glory the Lord deserves;
*   Bring a gift and come to God's court.*
Bow to the Lord in holy splendor;
*   Tremble before God, all the world. . . .*
Let sky and earth rejoice and shout;
*   Thunder, you sea and everything in you!*
Let the desert and everything in it rejoice;
*   Let all the trees of the forest sing*
Before the Lord. . . .

—Psalm 96: 1, 7, 9, 11-12, *The Psalms: A New Translation for Prayer and Worship,* translated by Gary Chamberlain, © 1984, The Upper Room. Used by permission.

Shout to the Lord, every land!
*   Be confident! Shout and sing!*
Sing to the Lord with a harp,
*   With a harp and the sound of music! . . .*

Storm, you ocean, and all that fills you,
*   You lands, and all who inhabit you.*
Clap your hands, great rivers;
*   You hills, all shout together*
Before the Lord. . . .

—Psalm 98:4-5, 7-8, *The Psalms: A New Translation for Prayer and Worship,* translated by Gary Chamberlain, © 1984, The Upper Room. Used by permission.

Praise the Lord! Hallelujah!
Praise God from the sky,
*   Praise God from the heights;*
Praise God, all you angels,
*   Praise God, heaven's armies.*
Praise God, sun and moon.

Praise God, all bright stars;
Praise God, skies above
*   And waters above the skies. . . .*

Praise the Lord from the earth,
*   Ocean deeps and dragons,*
Fire and hail, snow and smoke,
*   Gale wind doing God's word;*
All mountains and hills,
*   All fruit trees and cedars,*
All beasts, wild or tame,
*   Creeping things and soaring birds;*
All earth's kings and peoples,
*   All earth's princes and rulers,*
Young women and men,
*   And the old with the young.*
Praise the name of the Lord;
*   God alone is worthy of honor.*
God's might is above earth and sky;
*   God's people rise up in power.*
Israel's children are close to God,
*   God the glory of all faithful people!*
Praise the Lord! Hallelujah!

—Psalm 148:1-4, 7-14, *The Psalms: A New Translation for Prayer and Worship,* translated by Gary Chamberlain, © 1984, The Upper Room. Used by permission.

Praise God in the earthly temple;
*   Praise God in heaven's great dome.*
Praise God the mighty hero;
*   Praise God, supremely great.*
Praise God with blasting trumpets;
*   Praise God with harps and lyres.*
Praise God with drums and dancing;
*   Praise God with strings and flutes.*

Praise God with sounding cymbals;
Praise God with clamorous joy.
Let all who breathe, praise the Lord.
Praise the Lord, Hallelujah!

—Psalm 150, *The Psalms: A New Translation for*
Prayer and Worship, translated by Gary Chamberlain,
© 1984, The Upper Room. Used by permission.

In those moments when we have nothing to ask and everything to give, we know what *glory* and *glorify* mean!

We are God's *images* and *imagers.* We are changed into God's likeness, transformed into God's character. We are God's reflectors. "Glory" has to do with reflecting, imaging, mirroring—as the moon reflects the sun. Praising and reflecting God is the goal of the spiritual life—of human life. Giving God the central place in our lives and in our world. Making space for God who made space for us. As the moon reflects the sun, so the people of God are to reflect God. God is reflected in a people who live and love and laugh and talk and suffer and die in the sunshine of God's grace. We are God's self-revelation.

That's a tall order. It is made possible by Jesus Christ, at whose birth the angels sang:

"Glory to God in the highest heaven,
and on earth peace among those whom he favors."

—Luke 2:14, NRSV

The apostle John tells us that the glory of God shone in this Jesus, who from the beginning

was the Word, and the Word was with God, and the Word
was God. . . . In him was life, and the life was the light of
all people. The light shines in the darkness, and the dark-
ness did not overcome it. . . . The true light, which
enlightens everyone, was coming into the world. . . . And
the Word became flesh and lived among us, and we have

seen his glory, the glory as of a father's only son, full of
grace and truth. . . . From his fullness we have all
received, grace upon grace.

—Excerpts from John 1:1-16, NRSV

When John wrote those words he may have been remembering that splendid experience when he, along with Peter and James, accompanied Jesus to the hills to pray.

And while he was praying the appearance of his [Jesus']
face changed and his clothes became dazzling white. Sud-
denly there were two men talking with him; these were
Moses and Elijah, who appeared in glory and spoke of his
departure, the destiny he was to fulfil in Jerusalem.
Meanwhile Peter and his companions had been in a deep
sleep; but when they awoke, they saw his glory and the
two men who stood beside him. And as these were moving
away from Jesus, Peter said to him, "Master, how good it
is that we are here! Shall we make three shelters, one for
you, one for Moses, and one for Elijah?"; but he spoke
without knowing what he was saying. The words were
still on his lips when there came a cloud which cast a
shadow over them; they were afraid as they entered the
cloud, and from it came a voice: "This is my Son, my Cho-
sen; listen to him." When the voice had spoken, Jesus was
seen to be alone. The disciples kept silence and at that time
told nobody anything of what they had seen.

—Luke 9:29-36, NEB

Jesus was transformed. Something happened that has remained a mysterious yet majestic event for the life of Jesus' disciples ever since. At the birth of Jesus the glory of God showed itself in a human being. The glory of God took the form of a servant. At the transfiguration the servant exhibited the form of God. His Godness shone through his humanness.

For a moment, all doubts about Jesus were removed for the disciples. They were knocked breathless by a powerful Presence of God. "This is my Son!" The holy, separate, pure, majestic glory of God present in the common, the human, fraternizing with the unclean—Godness crammed into the earthly. The God who led people out of slavery and dried up the sea so they could pass through, the God who gave people food from heaven—this awesome, holy God says: "This is my Son." The divine in the human; the human in touch with the divine.

The luminous cloud, which to Jews meant the glory, the splendor, the excellence of God, enveloped them all. The disciples feared the thrust of God's Godness—the Presence of God. They believed that if they "saw" the glory of God, "saw" God, they would be consumed—it would blind them—they would die. Now the disciples "saw his glory" and they lived!

> The history of Jesus makes it really clear, for the first time, that God glorifies Himself not at the expense of men, but for their good. His glory means our life, our salvation, our abundance. . . . The glory of Jesus Christ is revealed because He is God in action, with decisive saving effects.[4]

The story ends with that marvelous sentence: "When the voice had spoken, Jesus was seen to be alone." Just Jesus alone. Just a human being. Just Jesus, like he was before. Or was he the same? Iraneus once said: "The glory of God is a person fully alive." The disciples could have seen it earlier, if they'd known what to look for. The transfiguration gave them a better glimpse of this person fully alive to God. They could see that he was more than just a human being.

What can we do with such an experience? The disciples were reduced to silence. Maybe that's all human beings can do with moments of insight, enlightenment, moments in which life seems to fit together, our goals seem clear, and God is near. Maybe we must accept such moments with awe, relish them, remember them, and let them be the focus of our lives.

Peter wanted to preserve the experience by doing nothing but admire it. We might do better if we followed the glory of God as he comes down from the mountain right into the darkness of human life. The light of the world comes so we can live in the light even when there is darkness; so we can listen to the small voice of God even in chaos; so we can have hope even in despair.

> When they came back to the disciples they saw a large crowd surrounding them and lawyers arguing with them. As soon as they saw Jesus the whole crowd were overcome with awe, and they ran forward to welcome him. He asked them, "What is this argument about?" A man in the crowd spoke up: "Master, I brought my son to you. He is possessed by a spirit which makes him speechless. Whenever it attacks him, it dashes him to the ground, and he foams at the mouth, grinds his teeth, and goes rigid. I asked your disciples to cast it out, but they failed." Jesus answered: "What an unbelieving and perverse generation! How long shall I be with you? How long must I endure you? Bring him to me." So they brought the boy to him; and as soon as the spirit saw him it threw the boy into convulsions, and he fell on the ground and rolled about foaming at the mouth. Jesus asked his father, "How long has he been like this?" "From childhood," he replied; "often it has tried to make an end of him by throwing him into the fire or into water. But if it is at all possible for you, take pity upon us and help us." "If it is possible!" said Jesus. "Everything is possible to one who has faith." "I have faith," cried the boy's father; "help me where faith falls short." Jesus saw then that the crowd was closing in upon them, so he rebuked the unclean spirit. "Deaf and dumb spirit," he said, "I command you, come out of him and never go back!" After crying aloud and racking him fiercely, it came out; and the boy looked like a corpse; in fact, many said, "He is dead." But Jesus took his hand and raised him to his feet, and he stood up.

The light of the world (John 8:12) came down into the darkness of disappointment, into the failure of faith, into the threat of evil and death that was tearing the boy apart—as it tears our world and ourselves apart. Jesus entered the situation boldly, confronting the chaos that convulses our world. He brought the glory of God down from the mountain into the life of the boy, his parents, and the people—and "they were all struck with awe at the majesty of God" (Luke 9:43, NEB). The boy was transformed. So were the father, the confused crowd, and the disappointed disciples.

We can get in on that transformation too. We get in on the glory of God by faith. "Everything is possible to one who has faith" (Mark 9:23, NEB). We need that faith so that the glory, the Godness, can come into us, to heal us, encourage us, and transform us. Christ's transformation is a staggering experience. It is also staggering to realize that *we too can be transformed.* Everything is possible to those who have faith— even a little faith. Let the light in a crack and you can be flooded with the glory of God. The glory of God is a person fully alive—like Christ—like we can be! The glory of Christ can shine through us.

> *"I have glorified thee on earth by completing the work which thou gavest me to do; and now, Father, glorify me in thy own presence with the glory which I had with thee before the world began. I have made thy name known to those thou didst give me out of the world. They were thine, thou gavest them to me, and they have obeyed thy command. . . . They have had faith to believe that thou didst send me. I pray for them; I am not praying for the world but for those whom thou hast given me, because*

> *they belong to thee. All that is mine is thine, and what is thine is mine; and through them has my glory shone."*
>
> —John 17:4-6, 8-10, NEB

This glory is the goal of the spiritual life. For John Calvin the question of the Christian life was not only "that most pregnant of all questions: what shall I do to be saved? . . . [which he] answers as Lutheranism answers it. But the great question that presses upon [Calvinism] is, How shall God be glorified?"[5] "For Calvin the ultimate end of history was not the salvation of man, but the glory of God."[6] Salvation means giving God back the central place in our lives and in the life of the world—making space for God.

"This is my Father's glory, that you may bear fruit in plenty and so be my disciples. As the Father has loved me, so I have loved you. Dwell in my love. . . . This is my commandment: love one another, as I have loved you" (John 15:8-12, NEB). All our works and our words, our play and creativity, has a goal. As artists of our lives we have a theme for our song, a motif for our painting, a point for our poem, a focus for our lives—the glory of God. "Whatever you do, do everything for the glory of God" (1 Cor. 10:31, NRSV).

> *God already has glory. . . . To give God glory only means that we recognize and honor Him in the excellence He displays by His terrific acts of liberation, recognize and honor Him by means of the obedience and festivity His glory elicits from us. His glory, just as His name, needs people who are willing (and who dare) to lose themselves in it—people who believe that to live is to celebrate the glory of God!*[7]

All ways of recognizing God's gifts and actions, all gestures of gratitude, all worship, prayer, compassion, and justice come together in glorifying God. For those who belong to God, the goal is glory.

FOOTNOTES

1. Kuitert, *Signals from the Bible*, 93.
2. Some of the thoughts expressed in the next few paragraphs reflect an unpublished lecture on 1 Peter given by Andrew Kuyvenhoven at the Christian Reformed Ministers' Institute, June, 1971; and two devotional writings by him in *Daylight*, November 9 and December 26.
3. Smedes, "Theology and the Playful Life," *God and the Good*, 58.
4. Kuitert, 94.
5. Williams, *The Descent of the Dove*, 174.
6. Richard, *The Spirituality of John Calvin*, 114.
7. Kuitert, 94-95.

WINDOWS
TO INSIGHT

View from St. Paul's

—Vincent Van Gogh

187

PSALM 29

Give to the Lord, you creatures of heaven,
*   Give to the Lord all glory and power.*
Give to the Lord a glorious name;
*   Bow down to the Lord in holy splendor.*

The voice of the Lord sounds over the oceans—
*   Crashing thunder above the deep seas.*
The voice of the Lord is power;
*   The voice of the Lord is splendor.*
The voice of the Lord splits the cedars;
*   God splinters the cedars of Lebanon.*
God makes Lebanon skip like a calf,
*   Mount Hermon skip like a wild young ox.*

Slashing the sky with lightning-swords,
*   The Lord's voice makes the desert writhe;*
*   The desert of Kadesh quakes.*
In terror, the deer flee God's thunder,
*   That snaps the limbs from the trees;*
*   In the temple God's glory appears!*

The throne of the Lord is above sky and sea;
*   The Lord will rule forever.*
Lord, give strength to your people;
*   Lord, bless your people with peace.*

—The Psalms: A New Translation for Prayer and Worship,
translated by Gary Chamberlain, © 1984,
The Upper Room. Used by permission.

THE SONG OF THE THREE (verses 35-39)
Apocryphal book that is added between Daniel 3:23 and 3:24

Bless the Lord, all you works of the Lord.
Praise and exalt the Lord above all forever.
Angels of the Lord, bless the Lord.
You heavens, bless the Lord.
All you waters above the heavens, bless the Lord.
All you hosts of the Lord, bless the Lord.
Sun and moon, bless the Lord.
Stars of heaven, bless the Lord.

Every shower and dew, bless the Lord.
All you winds, bless the Lord.
Fire and heat, bless the Lord.
Cold and chill, bless the Lord.
Dew and rain, bless the Lord.
Frost and chill, bless the Lord.
Ice and snow, bless the Lord.
Nights and days, bless the Lord.
Light and darkness, bless the Lord.
Lightnings and clouds, bless the Lord.

Let the earth bless the Lord.
Praise and exalt our God above all forever.
Mountains and hills, bless the Lord.
Everything growing from the earth, bless the Lord.
You springs, bless the Lord.
Seas and rivers, bless the Lord.
You dolphins and all water creatures, bless the Lord.
All you people, bless the Lord.

O Israel, bless the Lord.
Praise and exalt the Lord above all forever.

GOD'S GLORY

In those days a decree went out from Emperor Augustus that all the world should be registered. This was the first registration and was taken while Quirinius was governor of Syria. All went to their own towns to be registered. Joseph also went from the town of Nazareth in Galilee to Judea, to the city of David called Bethlehem, because he was descended from the house and family of David. He went to be registered with Mary, to whom he was engaged and who was expecting a child. While they were there, the time came for her to deliver her child. And she gave birth to her firstborn son and wrapped him in bands of cloth, and laid him in a manger, because there was no place for them in the inn.

In that region there were shepherds living in the fields, keeping watch over their flock by night. Then an angel of the Lord stood before them, and the glory of the Lord shone around them, and they were terrified. But the angel said to them, "Do not be afraid; for see—I am bringing you good news of great joy for all the people: to you is born this day in the city of David a Savior, who is the Messiah, the Lord. This will be a sign for you: you will find a child wrapped in bands of cloth and lying in a manger." And suddenly there was with the angel a multitude of the heavenly host, praising God and saying,

"Glory to God in the highest heaven,
and on earth peace among those whom he favors!"

—Luke 2:1-14, NRSV

Arise, shine; for your light has come
and the glory of the LORD has risen upon you.
For darkness shall cover the earth,
and thick darkness the peoples;
but the LORD will arise upon you,
and his glory will appear over you.
Nations shall come to your light,
and kings to the brightness of your dawn.

—Isaiah 60:1-3, NRSV

THE LIGHT OF THE WORLD

In the beginning was the Word, and the Word was with God, and the Word was God. He was in the beginning with God. All things came into being through him, and without him not one thing came into being. What has come into being in him was life, and the life was the light of all people. The light shines in the darkness, and the darkness did not overcome it.

There was a man sent from God whose name was John. He came as a witness to testify to the light, so that all might believe through him. He himself was not the light, but he came to testify to the light. The true light, which enlightens everyone, was coming into the world.

He was in the world, and the world came into being through him, yet the world did not know him. He came to what was his own, and his own people did not accept him. But to all who received him, who believed in his name, he gave power to become children of God, who were born, not of blood or of the will of the flesh or of the will of man, but of God.

And the Word became flesh and lived among us, and we have seen his glory, the glory as of a father's only son, full of grace and truth.

—John 1:1-14, NRSV

Again, Jesus spoke to them, saying, "I am the light of the world. Whoever follows me will never walk in darkness but will have the light of life."

—John 8:12, NRSV

You are the light of the world. A city built on a hill cannot be hid. No one after lighting a lamp puts it under the bushel basket but on the lampstand, and it gives light to all in the house. In the same way, let your light shine before others, so that they may see your good works and give glory to your Father in heaven.

—Matthew 5:14-16, NRSV

We declare to you what was from the beginning, what we have heard, what we have seen with our eyes, what we have looked at and touched with our hands, concerning the word of life—this life was revealed, and we have seen it and testify to it, and declare to you the eternal life that was with the Father and was revealed to us—we declare to you what we have seen and heard so that you also may have fellowship with us; and truly our fellowship is with the Father and with his Son Jesus Christ. We are writing these things so that our joy may be complete.

This is the message we have heard from him and proclaim to you, that God is light and in him there is no darkness at all. If we say that we have fellowship with him while we are walking in darkness, we lie and do not do what is true; but if we walk in the light as he himself is in the light, we have fellowship with one another, and the blood of Jesus his Son cleanses us from all sin.

—1 John 1:1-7, NRSV

Jesus Christ Preaching

—Rembrandt

HOLY, HOLY, HOLY!

Holy, holy, holy! Lord God Almighty!
Early in the morning our song shall rise to thee;
holy, holy, holy! merciful and mighty,
God in three persons, blessed Trinity!

Holy, holy, holy! All the saints adore thee,
casting down their golden crowns around the glassy sea;
cherubim and seraphim falling down before thee,
who wert and art and evermore shalt be.

Holy, holy, holy! Though the darkness hide thee,
though the eye made blind by sin thy glory may not see;
only thou art holy; there is none beside thee,
perfect in power, in love, and purity.

Holy, holy, holy! Lord God Almighty!
All thy works shall praise thy name, in earth and sky and sea;
holy, holy, holy! merciful and mighty,
God in three persons, blessed Trinity!

—Reginald Heber, 1827, alt.

O MIGHTY GOD

O mighty God, when I behold the wonder
Of all the world so gloriously arrayed—
The sun and moon and every star up yonder,
And all the things Thy mighty hand hath made:

Refrain
My soul is filled with singing, Lord, to Thee.
O mighty God, great is Thy love.
My soul is filled with singing, Lord, to Thee.
O mighty God, great is Thy love.

O loving God, when I behold a forest
And know that Thou hast planted every tree,
In memory's eye I see a tree on Calvary
Where Thy dear Son was crucified for me.
Refrain

When mists of time have like a vapor vanished
And all the saints are gathered 'round the throne,
We'll sing Thy praise while ages roll unending,
And worship Him who did for sin atone.
Refrain

—Carl Boberg, 1859-1940

GOD-GLORIFIERS

Glorifying God. *Our creation and election, we are told, are to the "praise of the glory of his grace" (Eph. 1:6). The end of man, we learn from the catechism, is to glorify God and to enjoy him forever. In its most basic terms, man's failure is his refusal to give God the glory and glorifying the creature instead (Rom. 1:25).*

Now, one condition for glorifying the excellence of the Creator is that his excellence be manifest. Where is it to be seen? Why, says the sometimes anti-playful Calvin, all around us. Little things and big things alike throw a floodlight on their Maker's splendid features. Doxologies are not only for the elite who are competent for contemplative visions: "even the common folk and the most untutored cannot be unaware of the excellence of the divine art . . . they cannot open their eyes without being compelled to witness it" (Inst., I.v.2). But even here, God is playfully disguising his glory, hiding it behind insects and lizards, as well as letting it shine more plainly from comets and suns. And we are told, as it were, to stand still, be receptively unproductive, and be awed by what we see. We are guests in the theater, and are privileged to know the star.

The act of God-glorifying is not very productive. We do not get great things done on earth by applauding God. This may be why some Calvinists are not sympathetic with a worship that accents God-applauding. Authentic praise, they tend to say, comes from the labors of our hands; God is praised by the good work done by stewards of his creation. There is no denying this, of course. But the biblical examples tend to correspond favorably to the summons of the Psalmist: "Praise him with trumpet sound; . . . with lute and harp! Praise him with timbrel and dance; . . . with strings and pipe! Praise him with sounding cymbals . . . with loud clashing cymbals" (Ps. 150:3-5).

It took me a long time to like the notion of being a God-glorifier. I didn't like a God who created human beings just to hear their applause. I had a juvenile fantasy of a narcissistic deity, liking what he saw in the mirror, but hungry for rave reviews. The Lord later gave me better insights into the playfulness of being a God-glorifier. One learns theology in many ways. For instance, I went to a concert not long ago to hear a great violinist perform. It was a splendid concert. Afterwards, we in the audience did our own "playing"; we applauded and applauded and applauded. The violinist bowed and left the stage. We would bring him back by applauding and yelling "Bravo!" He would come back, obviously enjoying every decibel, and then retire again. Then we would bring him back with our doxology. He let *us play with him. As this game was going on, we were all taken out of ourselves, in a kind of ecstasy, in a game we all played together. And I thought: glorifying God can be a wonderful game to play.*

—Lewis B. Smedes, "Theology and the Playful Life,"
God and the Good, pp. 57-58

A WORD ABOUT PRAISING

The most obvious fact about praise—whether of God or any-thing—strangely escaped me. I thought of it in terms of compli-ment, approval, or the giving of honour. I had never noticed that all enjoyment spontaneously overflows into praise unless (sometimes even if) shyness or the fear of boring others is deliberately brought in to check it. The world rings with praise—lovers praising their mistresses, readers their favourite poet, walkers praising the coun-tryside, players praising their favourite game—praise of weather, wines, dishes, actors, motors, horses, colleges, countries, historical personages, children, flowers, mountains, rare stamps, rare beetles, even sometimes politicians or scholars. I had not noticed how the humblest, and at the same time most balanced and capacious, minds praise most, while the cranks, misfits and malcontents praised least. . . . Except where intolerably adverse circumstances interfere, praise almost seems to be inner health made audible. . . . I had not noticed either that just as men spontaneously praise what-ever they value, so they spontaneously urge us to join them in praising it: "Isn't she lovely? Wasn't it glorious? Don't you think that magnificent?" The Psalmists in telling everyone to praise God are doing what all men do when they speak of what they care about. . . .

I think we delight to praise what we enjoy because the praise not merely expresses but completes the enjoyment; it is its appointed consummation. It is not out of compliment that lovers keep on telling one another how beautiful they are; the delight is incomplete till it is expressed. It is frustrating to have discovered a new author and not to be able to tell anyone how good he is; to come suddenly, at the turn of the road, upon some mountain valley of unexpected grandeur and then to have to keep silent because the people with you care for it no more than for a tin can in the ditch; to hear a good joke and find no one to share it with. . . . This is so even when our expressions are inadequate, as of course they usually are. But how if one could really and fully praise even such things to perfection—utterly "get out" in poetry or music or paint the upsurge of appre-ciation which almost bursts you? Then indeed the object would be fully appreciated and our delight would have attained perfect development. The worthier the object, the more intense this delight would be. If it were possible for a created soul fully (I mean, up to the full measure conceivable in a finite being) to "appreciate," that is to love and delight in, the worthiest object of all, and simultane-ously at every moment to give this delight perfect expression, then that soul would be in supreme beatitude. It is along these lines that I find it easiest to understand the Christian doctrine that

"Heaven" is a state in which angels now, and people hereafter, are perpetually employed in praising God. . . . To see what the doctrine really means, we must suppose ourselves to be in perfect love with God—drunk with, drowned in, dissolved by, that delight which, far from remaining pent up within ourselves as incommunicable, hence hardly tolerable, bliss, flows out from us incessantly again in effortless and perfect expression, our joy no more separable from the praise in which it liberates and utters itself than the brightness a mirror receives is separable from the brightness it sheds. The Scotch catechism says that man's chief end is "to glorify God and enjoy Him forever." But we shall then know that these are the same thing. Fully to enjoy is to glorify. In commanding us to glorify Him, God is inviting us to enjoy Him.

Meanwhile of course we are merely, as Donne says, tuning our instruments. The tuning up of the orchestra can be itself delightful, but only to those who can in some measure, however little, antici-pate the symphony. . . . When we carry out our "religious duties" we are like people digging channels in a waterless land, in order that when at last the water comes, it may find them ready. I mean, for the most part. There are happy moments, even now, when a trickle creeps along the dry beds; and happy the souls to whom this happens often.

—C. S. Lewis, *Reflections on the Psalms*, pp. 93-97

195

HONOR AND GLORY AND PRAISE

*I looked, and there before my eyes was a door opened in heaven. . . .
There in heaven stood a throne, and on the throne sat one whose
appearance was like the gleam of jasper and cornelian; and round
the throne was a rainbow, bright as an emerald. In a circle about
this throne were twenty-four other thrones, and on them sat
twenty-four elders, robed in white and wearing crowns of gold.
From the throne went out flashes of lightning and peals of thunder.
Burning before the throne were seven flaming torches, the seven
spirits of God, and in front of it stretched what seemed a sea of
glass, like a sheet of ice.*

*In the centre, round the throne itself, were four living creatures,
covered with eyes, in front and behind. The first creature was like a
lion, the second like an ox, the third had a human face, the fourth
was like an eagle in flight. The four living creatures, each of them
with six wings, had eyes all over, inside and out; and by day and by
night without a pause they sang: "Holy, holy, holy is God the sov-
ereign Lord of all, who was, and is and is to come!" As often as the
living creatures give glory and honour and thanks to the One who
sits on the throne, who lives for ever and ever, the twenty-four
elders fall down before the One who sits on the throne and worship
him who lives for ever and ever; and as they lay their crowns before
the throne they cry: "Thou art worthy, O Lord our God, to receive
glory and honour and power, because thou didst create all things;
by thy will they were created, and have their being!" . . . "Worthy is
the Lamb, the Lamb that was slain, to receive all power and wealth,
wisdom and might, honour and glory and praise!"*

—Revelation 4:1-11; 5:12, NEB

Orchard in
Provence

—Vincent Van Gogh

197

EXERCISES

In Session

Contemplate the account of the transfiguration of Christ.

1. Read the story from Luke 9:28-36.
2. Spend fifteen minutes in silence, imagining yourself as a disciple who is witnessing this event. Focus especially on what is happening to Jesus. What are your impressions, your feelings, as you watch him being transformed? Jot notes in your journal, if you wish.
3. End this meditation by repeating for two minutes, very slowly, "I belong to God, glory to God."
4. Take five minutes to write a prayer of praise, based on your experience. Please be ready to share your ideas and prayer with others.

At Home

1. Continue to practice your personal prayer discipline, including intercessory petitions for those in need of justice and compassion. Think about changes, if any, you might want to make in your prayer discipline. Perhaps you can get together with others from the group to discuss this and to encourage each other.
2. When you use the phrase "I belong to God," you might add the words "glory to God." Thus, the prayer becomes:
   I belong to God,
   Glory to God.
3. Take time to read chapter 9. If you have found readings from previous chapters that were particularly helpful to you, consider rereading them this week.

These are the last exercises. They were intended not as an end in themselves but as a means to expand the possibilities of prayer in your life and to enrich your praying. Through all your reading and reflecting, talking and silence, meditating and thinking, I hope you have learned to pray more and more deeply; that you have found some profoundly precious space for God in your life.

I encourage you to continue using and developing your discipline of prayer until praying becomes as natural for you as breathing. Prayer is the breath of the spiritual life.

May your continued praying connect you with the very Breath—the Spirit—of God, who gives life and peace and vigor and enormous joy. To whom be the glory forever. Amen.

BIBLIOGRAPHY

BATTLES, FORD LEWIS. *The Piety of John Calvin.* Grand Rapids, Mich.: Baker Book House, 1978.

BEUCHNER, FREDERICK. *The Magnificent Defeat.* New York: The Seabury Press, Inc., 1966.

BONHOEFFER, DIETRICH. *Life Together.* New York: Harper and Row, Publishers, Inc., 1954.

———. *Psalms: The Prayer Book of the Bible.* Minneapolis: Augsburg Publishing House, 1970.

BOULDIN, LAWRENCE M. "Contemplation and Action." *The NICM Journal,* vol. 2, No. 2 (1977), pp. 23-25.

BOYD, MALCOLM. *Are You Running with Me, Jesus?* New York: Holt, Rinehart and Winston, 1965.

BUTEYN, DONALD P. "Spirituality, Piety and Conflict." *Pacific Theological Review,* Fall, 1981, p. 10.

CALLAHAN, WILLIAM R. *Noisy Contemplation.* Hyattsville, MD: Quixote Center, 1983.

CALVIN, JOHN. *Institutes of the Christian Religion,* vol. III. Translated by John Allen. Grand Rapids, Mich.: Wm. B. Eerdmans Publishing Co., 1949.

———. *Institution of the Christian Religion.* 1536 Edition. Translated by Ford Lewis Battles. Atlanta: John Knox Press, 1975.

———. "The Catechism of the Church of Geneva," *Tracts and Treatises,* vol. 2. Translated by Henry Beveridge. Grand Rapids, Mich.: Wm. B. Eerdmans Publishing Co., 1958.

CHAMBERLAIN, Gary. *The Psalms: A New Translation for Prayer and Worship.* Nashville: The Upper Room, 1984.

CHARITON, IGUMEN OF VALAMO, comp. *The Art of Prayer.* (An Orthodox Anthology.) Translated by E. Kadloubovsky and E. M. Palmer. London and Boston: Faber & Faber, 1978.

CUMMINGS, E. E. *Complete Poems 1913-1962,* vol. 2. New York: Harcourt Brace, Inc., 1947.

EDWARDS, TILDEN. *Living Simply Through the Day, Spiritual Survival in a Complex Age.* New York: Paulist Press, 1977.

ELIOT, T. S. "Choruses from 'The Rock,' " from *Collected Poems 1909-1935.* New York: Harcourt Brace, Inc., 1936.

FEDOTOV, G. P., ed. *A Treasury of Russian Spirituality.* London: Sheed & Ward, Ltd., 1977.

FOSTER, RICHARD. *The Celebration of Discipline.* San Francisco: Harper and Row, Publishers, Inc., 1978.

FOX, MATTHEW, O. P. *Whee, Wee, We—All the Way Home. A Guide to the New Sensual Spirituality.* Wilmington, NC: A Consortium Book, 1976.

FROST, ROBERT. "Death of a Hired Man." *Robert Frost's Poems.* New York: Pocketbooks, Inc., 1954.

GELINEAU, JOSEPH. Introduction to *The Psalms, A New Translation (Singing Version).* New York: Paulist Press, 1968.

GREELY, ANDREW M. *The Great Mysteries: An Essential Catechism.* New York: The Seabury Press, Inc. A Crossroad Book, 1976.

GREEN, ARTHUR, and BARRY HOLTZ, eds. and trans. *Your Word Is Fire: The Hasidic Masters on Contemplative Prayer.* Ramsey, NJ: Paulist Press, 1977.

Hymns for the Living Church. Carol Stream, IL: Hope Publishing Co., 1974.

KELSEY, MORTON. *The Other Side of Silence, A Guide to Christian Meditation.* Ramsey, NJ: Paulist Press, 1976.

KELTY, MATTHEW. *Flute Solo, Reflections of a Trappist Hermit.* Garden City, NY: Doubleday & Co., Inc., Image Books, 1980.

KREEFT, PETER J. *Heaven, the Heart's Deepest Longing.* San Francisco: Harper and Row, Publishers, 1980.

KUITERT, HARRY M. *Signals from the Bible.* Translated by Lewis B. Smedes. Grand Rapids, Mich.: Wm. B. Eerdmans Publishing Co., 1972.

KUYPER, ABRAHAM. *To Be Near unto God.* Grand Rapids, Mich.: Baker Book House, 1979.

KUYVENHOVEN, ANDREW. *Daylight.* Jordan Station, Ont.: Paideia Press, 1977.

L'ENGLE, MADELEINE. *The Weather of the Heart.* Wheaton, IL: Harold Shaw Publications, 1978.

LAMB, JOHN ALEXANDER. *The Psalms in Christian Worship.* London: The Faith Press, 1962.

LEECH, KENNETH. *True Prayer, An Invitation to Christian Spirituality.* San Francisco: Harper and Row, Publishers, 1980.

LEWIS, C. S. *Reflections on the Psalms.* New York: Harcourt Brace, Inc., 1964.

McDONNELL, THOMAS P., ed. *A Thomas Merton Reader.* Garden City, NY: Doubleday & Co., Inc., Image Books, 1974.

McNEILL, DONALD P.; DOUGLAS A. MORRISON; HENRI J. M. NOUWEN. *Compassion: A Reflection on the Christian Life.* Garden City, NY: Doubleday & Co., Inc., 1982.

MERTON, THOMAS. *The Climate of Monastic Prayer.* Kalamazoo, Mich.: Cistercian Publications, 1971.

———. *The Wisdom of the Desert.* New York: A New Directions Book, 1970.

———. *Thoughts in Solitude.* New York: Farrar, Straus and Giroux Inc., 1974.

METZ, JOHANN BAPTIST, and KARL RAHNER. *The Courage to Pray.* New York: Crossroad Publishing Co., 1981.

NOMURA, YUSHI. *Desert Wisdom: Sayings from the Desert Fathers.* Garden City, NY: Doubleday & Co., Inc., 1982.

NOUWEN, HENRI J. M. *Clowning in Rome*. Garden City, NY: Doubleday & Co., Inc., Image Books, 1979.

———. *Reaching Out*. Garden City, NY: Doubleday & Co., Inc., 1975.

———. *The Genesee Diary*. Garden City, NY: Doubleday & Company, Inc., 1976.

———. *The Living Reminder*. New York: The Seabury Press, Inc., 1977.

———. *The Way of the Heart*. New York: The Seabury Press, Inc., 1981.

———. *The Wounded Healer*. Garden City, NY: Doubleday & Co., Inc., 1972.

OATES, WAYNE E. *Nurturing Silence in a Noisy Heart*. Garden City, NY: Doubleday & Co., Inc., 1979.

OLD, HUGHES OLIPHANT. *Praying with the Bible*. Philadelphia: The Geneva Press, 1980.

———. "Daily Prayer in the Reformed Church of Strasbourg, 1525-1530," *Worship*. March 1978.

———. "Meditation in Calvin's Commentary on the Psalms," unpublished paper, 1977.

———. "The Psalms as Christian Prayer: A Preface to the Liturgical Use of the Psalter," unpublished paper.

PIPER, JOSEF. *Leisure, The Basis of Culture*. Translated by Alexander Dru. New York: Pantheon Books, a Division of Random House, Inc., 1963.

The Psalms: A New Translation. Philadelphia: The Westminster Press, 1963.

Psalter Hymnal. Grand Rapids, Mich.: Board of Publications of the Christian Reformed Church, 1959.

Psalter Hymnal. Grand Rapids, Mich.: CRC Publications, 1987.

Psalter Hymnal Supplement. Grand Rapids, Mich.: Christian Reformed Board of Publications, 1974.

RAHNER, KARL. *Encounters with Silence*. Westminster, MD: The Newman Press, 1968.

RICHARD, LUCIAN JOSEPH. *The Spirituality of John Calvin*. Atlanta: John Knox Press, 1974.

SEERVELD, CALVIN. *Take Hold of God and Pull*. Toronto: Wedge Publishing Foundation, 1972.

SMEDES, LEWIS B. *A Pretty Good Person*. San Francisco, CA: Harper and Row, Publishers, 1990.

———. "Suffering: The Christian Style of Life," *The Reformed Journal*, February 1969, p. 12.

SMEDES, LEWIS B., and CLIFTON J. ORLEBEKE, eds. *God and the Good*. Grand Rapids, Mich.: Wm. B. Eerdmans Publishing Co., 1975.

SMITH, MARTIN L. *The Word Is Very Near You: A Guide to Praying with Scripture*. Boston, MA: Cowley Publications, 1989.

STEERE, DOUGLAS. *Prayer in the Contemporary World*. Wallingford, PA: Pendle Hill, 1966.

STEINDL-RAST, DAVID. *The Listening Heart: The Art of Contemplative Living*. New York: The Crossroad Publishing Company, 1981.

THIELICKE, HELMUT. *The Waiting Father*. New York: Harper and Row, Publishers, Inc., 1959.

VAN GOGH, VINCENT. *The Complete Letters of Vincent Van Gogh.* Boston: New York Graphic Society Books/ Little, Brown and Co., 1978.

VISSER 't HOOFT, W. A. *Rembrandt and the Gospel.* New York: Meridian Books, Inc., A Living Age Book, 1960.

WALLACE, RONALD. *Calvin's Doctrine of the Christian Life.* Grand Rapids, Mich.: Wm. B. Eerdmans Publishing Co., 1959.

WARD, BENEDICTA, trans. *The Sayings of the Desert Fathers.* Kalamazoo, Mich.: Cistercian Publications, 1975.

WARE, FR. KALLISTOS. *The Orthodox Way.* Crestwood, NY: St. Vladimir's Orthodox Theological Seminary, 1979.

WASKOW, ARTHUR I. *Godwrestling.* New York: Schocken Books, Inc., 1978.

WILDER, THORNTON. *Our Town* (A Play in Three Acts). A Perennial Classic. New York: Harper and Row, Publishers, Inc., 1968.

WILLIAMS, CHARLES. *The Descent of the Dove: A Short History of the Holy Spirit in the Church.* Grand Rapids, Mich.: Wm. B. Eerdmans Publishing Co., 1939.

WOLFF, PIERRE. *May I Hate God?* New York: Paulist Press, 1979.

ZYLSTRA, HENRY. *The Testament of Vision.* Grand Rapids, Mich.: Wm. B. Eerdmans Publishing Co., 1958.

ACKNOWLEDGMENTS

The Scripture quotations in this publication are from the New Revised Standard Version, ©1989 by the Division of Christian Education of the National Council of the Churches of Christ in the U.S.A., and used by permission; The New English Bible, © 1970 by the Oxford University Press and Cambridge University Press, and used by permission; *The Psalms: A New Translation,* © 1963 by The Grail, England, and used by permission of the Grail; and *The Psalms: A New Translation for Prayer and Worship,* translated by Gary Chamberlain, © 1984 by The Upper Room, Nashville, TN, and used by permission.

Excerpts from *The Complete Letters of Vincent Van Gogh* are reprinted by permission of New York Graphic Society Books/Little, Brown and Company, Boston. All rights reserved.

Excerpts from *Leisure, The Basis of Culture* by Josef Pieper. © 1963. Reprinted by permission of Pantheon Books, a Division of Random House, Inc.

Excerpts from *The Climate of Monastic Prayer* by Thomas Merton. © 1971 by Cistercian Publications, Kalamazoo, Mich. Used by permission.

Excerpts from *The Way of the Heart* by Henri J. M. Nouwen. © 1981 by Henri J. M. Nouwen. Used by permission of The Seabury Press.

Text and illustrations from *Desert Wisdom* by Yushi Nomura. © 1982 by Yushi Nomura. Reprinted by permission of Doubleday & Company, Inc.

Excerpts from *The Other Side of Silence* by Morton Kelsey. © 1976 by The Missionary Society of St. Paul the Apostle in the State of New York. Used by permission of Paulist Press.

Excerpts from *The Testament of Vision* by Henry Zylstra. © 1958, Wm. B. Eerdmans Publishing Company. Used by permission.

Excerpts from *The Piety of John Calvin* by Ford Lewis Battles. © 1978 by Baker Book House and used by permission.

Excerpts from *Reaching Out* by Henri J. M. Nouwen. © 1975 by Henri J. M. Nouwen. Reprinted by permission of Doubleday & Company, Inc., and William Collins Sons & Company Ltd., London.

ART CREDITS